The New Testament Church

by

Roy E. Cogdill

© **Guardian of Truth Foundation 2008.** All rights reserved. No part of this book may be reproduced in any form without written permission from the publisher. Printed in the United States of America.

ISBN 10: 1584270810

ISBN 13: 978-158427081-2

Guardian of Truth Foundation
P.O. Box 9670
Bowling Green, Kentucky 42102
1-800-428-0121
www.truthbooks.net

TABLE OF CONTENTS

PART ONE:	**The Nature of the Church**	**9**
Lesson 1	The Called Out Body	10
Lesson 2	The Household of God	12
Lesson 3	The Kingdom of God	14
Lesson 4	The Body of Christ	16
Lesson 5	The Temple of God	19
Lesson 6	The Vineyard of the Lord	21
PART TWO:	**The Origin of the Church**	**23**
Lesson 7	The Origin of the Church	24
Lesson 8	The Authority of the Church	27
Lesson 9	Use of Old Testament Scriptures	29
PART THREE:	**The Mission of the Church**	**31**
Lesson 10	Evangelism	32
Lesson 11	Personal Evangelism	34
Lesson 12	Edification	36
Lesson 13	Ministry to Poor	38
PART FOUR:	**Church Membership**	**41**
Lesson 14	The Grandeur and Glory of the Church	42
Lesson 15	What Membership Means	44
Lesson 16	Membership—Its Responsibilities	46
Lesson 17	Salvation and Church Membership	48
Lesson 18	How to Become a Member	50
PART FIVE:	**Church Government**	**53**
Lesson 19	The Organization of the Church	54
Lesson 20	The Eldership	56
Lesson 21	Deacons	58
Lesson 22	Evangelists	61

PART SIX:	**Unity**	**63**
Lesson 23	The Importance of Unity	64
Lesson 24	The Undenominational Character of the Church	67
Lesson 25	The Sin of Division	70
Lesson 26	God's Plan for Unity	72
Lesson 27	Unity, An Individual Obligation	75
PART SEVEN:	**The Identity of the Church**	**77**
Lesson 28	The Identity of the Church	78
Lesson 29	A Scriptural Name	81
Lesson 30	Scriptural Worship	84
Lesson 31	Scriptural Teaching	86
Lesson 32	Scriptural Teaching	89
Lesson 33	The Purity of the Church	91
Lesson 34	The Church and Worldliness	93
Lesson 35	The Discipline of the Church	95
PART EIGHT:	**The Worship of the Church**	**99**
Lesson 36	The Lord's Day	100
Lesson 37	The Lord's Supper	103
Lesson 38	Music in the Worship	106
Lesson 39	Instrumental Music	109
Lesson 40	Church Finances	113
Lesson 41	Church Finances	116
Lesson 42	Church Finances	118
PART NINE:	**Churches of the New Testament Era**	**121**
Lesson 43	The Church at Jerusalem	122
Lesson 44	The Church at Antioch	124
Lesson 45	The Corinthian Church	126
Lesson 46	The Church at Philippi	128
Lesson 47	The Church at Ephesus	130
Lesson 48	The Church at Thessalonica	134
Lesson 49	The Church at Rome	137
Lessons 50-52	A Study of the Seven Churches of Asia	140

Foreword

It is, of course, impossible to work over and refine such a series of lessons thoroughly enough to eliminate all the mistakes either in material or form. These lessons have been taught both by the author and others and many errors eliminated by their use. As they are used further other mistakes will be discovered. Teachers using these outlines are asked to watch for errors and call them to the attention of the publishers that they may be avoided in succeeding issues.

It is with the earnest hope and fervent prayer that they may help in the spreading "by the Church the manifold wisdom of God" (Eph. 3:10) that these lessons and outlines on "The New Testament Church" are introduced.

THE AUTHOR R. E. C.

PREFACE

Outlines and study series are nothing new. Many have appeared, and many have vanished because of their lack of usability. The outlines on "The New Testament Church" that appear on the following pages of this book are the results of careful and prayerful study with the purpose in mind to develop a series of lessons that would be practical and usable. They are offered in the hope that others will find them such a work.

In many of the lesson helps which have been so widely relied upon in the past, there is not the close use and dependence upon the Bible itself that there should be in such work. Instead of having the tendency to familiarize the student with the texts of the Bible itself there is the inclination to rely entirely upon the lesson helps and they are frequently studied without recourse to the scriptures themselves. The lessons in this series have been arranged with this need in mind, and the student or teacher will find it impossible either to prepare or recite the lessons taught by these outlines without going to the Bible to search out the truths and passages that teach the lessons implied. It is a firm conviction that such should be the case and that all times the Bible itself should be the text and our reliance placed entirely upon it. This book of outlines should serve as but a guidebook with the Bible as the text.

The Churches of Christ have steadily progressed in spite of ridicule and opposition until they have reached a plane of dignity and respectability in the world. They are now confronted with the danger of accepting their place among the religious bodies of the world and becoming merely ANOTHER DENOMINATION. It is quite commonly a subject of discussion that there is but little difference between the Church of Christ and other religious bodies. The purpose, prayer and aim in the preparation and development of these lessons have been to make the distinctive position occupied by the Church of Christ outstanding and easily discernible. Members, both young and old, need to know the difference between the Church and denominationalism. Indoctrination along this line is imperative if the members of the Churches of Christ are to remain "a people for God's own possession" (1 Pet. 2:9).

SUGGESTIONS TO TEACHER AND STUDENT

Let the Bible be your text and these outlines serve only as a guide in the study of the Bible. Supply yourself with a good Bible.

Keep your Bible at hand not only during the study and preparation of these lessons but also in the recitation period.

Make it a point to cover one lesson each class period. There are fifty-two outlines, one for each week of the year, and in a class that meets weekly, better results will be obtained if too much time is not spent on any one point but the lesson studied as a whole. Many of the questions that arise for discussion during recitation will be dealt with in subsequent lessons or a subsequent part of the same lesson. General discussion can best be invited after the lesson is first covered entirely.

The lessons are not burdened with questions for discussion. It has been an aim of this work to avoid sterotyped recitation. The questions that follow the lessons are for the purpose of helping to prepare the lesson as much as for class discussion.

If the teacher will urge the students to bring their Bibles to class and, during the class period, will have the passages which are cited read aloud, the best impressions will be made and the lesson will proceed more easily. Too, this will do much toward familiarizing the student with the text of the Bible, which today is very much needed. Many of the passages cited can be assigned at the beginning of the lesson and looked up beforehand and then at the proper time used to establish and emphasize the point at hand.

The greatest advantage will come from emphasizing what the Bible says on the point rather than permitting a free expression of opinions with reference to it.

PART FIRST
THE NATURE OF THE CHURCH

INTRODUCTION—Many descriptive phrases are applied to the Church in the New Testament scriptures. These phrases give emphasis to various features of the Church and set forth its nature. The first six lessons of this series concern these descriptive phrases applied to the Church and therefore constitute a study of The Nature of the Church. They should be studied with this idea in mind.

LESSON 1 _____	**THE CALLED OUT BODY**
LESSON 2 _____	**THE HOUSEHOLD OF GOD**
LESSON 3 _____	**THE KINGDOM OF GOD**
LESSON 4 _____	**THE BODY OF CHRIST**
LESSON 5 _____	**THE TEMPLE OF GOD**
LESSON 6 _____	**THE VINEYARD OF THE LORD**

LESSON 1
THE CALLED OUT BODY

INTRODUCTION—Many descriptive phrases are applied to the Church in New Testament scriptures. These phrases give emphasis to various features of the Church and set forth its nature. The first six lessons of this series concern these descriptive phrases applied to the Church and therefore constitute a study of The Nature of the Church. They should be studied with this idea in mind.

I. The Meaning of the Term "Church":
  A. Derived from *Kuriakos* meaning "of or belonging to the Lord."
  B. Translation of Greek term *ekklesia*—the actual term used by Jesus and apostles in New Testament.
  C. Literal meaning of term "to call out."
  D. The Church then in New Testament scriptures means "a called out body of people."
  E. Word "Church" used in two senses in the New Testament.
   1. Referring to all those called out of the world into God's service—universally (Matt. 16:18; Eph. 5:23-25).
   2. Referring to all those "called out" into God's service in any definite locality (1 Cor. 1:2; 1 Thess. 1:1).

II. The Nature of This Calling:
  A. Called of God—a divine calling (1 Pet. 5:10; 1 Cor. 7:15; 2 Tim. 1:7-9).
  B. Called into fellowship and peace of Christ—Into one Body (1 Cor. 1:9; Col. 3:15).
  C. Called to be children of God (Rom. 9:25-26; 1 John 3:1).
  D. Called to be saints (1 Cor. 1:2; Rom. 1:7).
  E. A holy calling (1 Thess. 4:7; 2 Tim. 1:9; 2 Pet. 1:15)
  F. A heavenly calling (Heb. 3:1).

III. How We Are Called:
  A. Made possible by suffering of Christ (2 Pet. 2:21).
  B. Out of darkness (2 Pet. 2:9).
  C. By the gospel of Christ (2 Thess. 2:13-14).

IV. The Hope of This Calling:
  A. That we may be worthy (2 Thess. 1:11-12; Eph. 4:1-3).
  B. To inherit a blessing (2 Pet. 3:9).
  C. Unto perfection (Phil. 3:13-16).
  D. Make our calling and election sure (2 Pet. 1:10).

Questions for Discussion:
1. What is the meaning of the word "church" as it is used in the New Testament scriptures? _____

2. In what two senses is it used? _____

3. Into whose service are we called? _____

4. What relationship with God is established as a result of our being called? ___

5. What character does this calling demand? _____

6. Through what medium are we called? (1) direct operation of the Holy Spirit; (2) prayer; or (3) preaching the Gospel? _____

7. What is the ultimate hope of our calling? _____

LESSON 2
"THE HOUSEHOLD OF GOD"

I. The Family Feature of the Church:
   A. The word "house" used to designate families (Acts 10:2: Heb. 11:7; Luke 1:27).
   B. Church referred to as House of God meaning Family of God (1 Tim. 3:15; Heb. 3:6; Eph. 2:19; 3:15).

II. Salient. Features of God's Family—the Church:
   A. God is the Father (Eph. 3:14; 4:6; Matt. 23:9; 1 Cor. 8:6).
   B. Christ, a son over the House of God (Heb. 3:6); Christians, his brethren (Heb. 2:12; Matt. 23:8; 25:40).
   C. All Christians are children of God:
      1. Sons and heirs (Rom. 8:15-16; Gal. 4:7); In Christ Jesus (Gal. 3:26).
      2. Children of God—Children of Devil (1 John 3:10).
      3. "Church of God the Father" (1 Thess. 1:1).
      4. Conclusion:
         a. All of God's children are in God's Family.
         b. God's Family is the Church.
         c. Therefore all of God's Children are in the Church.

III. Blessedness of This Relationship:
   A. Approach to God as Father (Matt. 6:6-9; Eph. 3:14).
   B. Christ our Great High Priest and advocate to plead our cause (Heb. 4:14; 10:21; 1 John 2:1).
   C. Holy Spirit to lead and guide us (Rom. 8:14).
      1. Receive Holy Spirit because we are sons (Gal. 4:6).
      2. To walk by Spirit (Gal. 5:16).
      3. Spirit is the Truth (John 1:17; 1 John 5:7).
   D. God's fatherly provision (Rom. 8:32; Jas. 1:17; Matt. 6:8, 33-34; 7:7-11).
   E. God's fatherly correction (Heb. 12:4-11).
   F. God's fatherly protection (Phil. 4:5-7; 1 Cor. 10:12-18).
   G. God's everpresent Love (1 John 3:1; Rom. 8:38-89).
   H. Heir of God (Rom. 8:17; Gal. 3:29: 1 Pet. 1:3-5).

IV. This Relationship Demands:
  A. Separation from world (2 Cor. 6:17-18; 7:1; 1 John 2:15-16).
  B. Obedient as children (1 John 3:10; 1 Pet. 1:14; Eph. 5:6; Rom. 8:12-17); walk not after flesh (1 John 1:6-7).
  C. Wear family name (Acts 4:11-12; 11:26; 1 Pet. 4:15-16; Col. 3:17).
  D. Love our brethren (1 John 4:7, 20-21; 3:13-19).

V. How We Become Children of God:
  A. By being born again (John 3:3-5).
  B. By faith and baptism (Gal. 3:26-27).
  C. By obedience to God's word (1 Pet. 1:22-23).

Questions for Discussion:
1. If the Church is God's family, how many churches does God have? _____

2. How many of God's children are in the Church? _____

3. What blessings are available to God's children? _____

4. How do we become children of God? _____

5. As children of God, how must we treat one another? _____

6. What position in God's family is accorded to Christ? _____

7. What is demanded of God's children? _____

8. Can a child of God be finally disinherited (1 Pet. 1:3-5)? _____

LESSON 3
THE KINGDOM OF GOD

I. In Government, God's Church is a Kingdom:
 A. Kingdom preached at hand (Matt. 3:2; Mark 1:14-15).
 B. Parables set forth Church as Kingdom (Matt. 13:24, 44, 45, 47).
 C. Apostles given authority in Kingdom (Matt. 16:18-19; 19:28).
 D. People alive in time of Christ were to witness coming of Kingdom (Mark 9:1; Luke 9:27; 12:31-32).
 E. A spiritual Kingdom—not earthly (John 18:36; Rom. 14: 17; 1 Cor. 4:20; Luke 17:20-21).
 F. After day of Pentecost and coming of Holy Spirit, Kingdom spoken of as in existence (Acts 8:12; 20:25; 28:23, 31; Col. 1:13; 1 Thess. 2:12).
 G. In coming unto the Church, we receive the Kingdom (Heb. 12:22-28).
 H. Lord's Supper is in the Kingdom (Luke 22:16-18; 29-30).

II. Christ as King:
 A. By his own teaching and acknowledgment (Luke 23:1-3; John 18:37).
 B. He conquered in becoming King (Heb. 2:9, 14-15; Rev. 1:18; 1 John 3:8; Matt. 12:24-29; Luke 11:17-22; 10:17-19).
 C. His territory (Luke 4:5-8) was wrested from Satan (Matt. 28:18-20; Rev. 1:5-9).
 D. His authority and throne (Luke 1:32-33; Eph. 1:18-23; 1 Tim. 6:15; 1 Pet. 3:22).
 E. His law (John 12:48; 1:17; 17:8; 1 Cor. 9:21; 1 John 4:6).

III. Essentials of Citizenship in God's Kingdom:
 A. Enter by new birth (John 3:5; Acts 2:36-41).
 B. Must do God's will (Matt. 7:21).
 C. Center affections on heavenly things (Phil. 3:12-15; Col. 3:1-4).
 E. Greatness in Kingdom measured by service rendered (Matt. 20:20-28).
 F. Must be united (Luke 11:17).
 G. Requires sacrifice (Mark 10:23-31).
 H. Receive as little child (Mark 10:15).

IV. The Final Picture (Matt. 13:36-43; 25:31-46; 2 Thess. 1:7-8, 10).

Questions for Discussion:

1. What feature of the Church is emphasized in the fact that it is a Kingdom? ___

2. What is the nature of this form of government? ___

3. Who is the King? How did he become King? ___

4. How complete is his power and authority? ___

5. How do we become citizens of Christ's Kingdom? ___

6. When did Christ become King (Eph. 1:18-19)? ___

7. What is the law in Christ's Kingdom? ___

8. Whose authority must be recognized exclusively in the Kingdom of Christ? ___

9. What are some of the obligations of citizenship? ___

10. How is success in the Kingdom measured? ___

11. What will become of those in the Kingdom who give offense? ___

12. Is the Kingdom of Christ spiritual or earthly (John 18:36)? ___

13. How extensive is Christ's dominion now (Rev. 1:5; 1 Pet. 3:22; Eph. 1:20-23)?

LESSON 4
THE BODY OF CHRIST

I. The Church Called the Body of Christ:
  A. Clearly emphasing our relationship to Christ and to fellow Christians.
   1. Church is His Body (Eph. 1:23).
   2. Body is the Church (Col. 1:18, 24).

II. The New Testament Teaches That There is One Body. This figure emphasizes the singularity of the Church:
   1. Many members—one body (Rom. 12:4-5); but one body (1 Cor. 12:20).
   2. Jew and Gentile reconciled in one body (Eph. 2:16).
   3. One Lord, one faith, one baptism, ONE BODY (Eph. 4:4-5).
   4. Conclusion: If there is but one spiritual Body of Christ and that is the Church—How many Churches of Christ are there?

III. Christ is the Head of His Spiritual Body—The Church (Col. 1:18; Eph. 1:23).
  A. His dominion over the Church is complete—"Head over all things to the Church which is His Body" (Eph. 1:23).
  B. Just as the members of one's physical body must be subject to his mind—so we must be subject to Christ in everything as members of His Body (Eph. 5:24).
   1. What the Head commands we can and must do.
   2. What He does not command and teach we must not do (2 John 9).
  C. From the Head come the impulses that strengthen and move the members of the Body in the performance of their work (Eph. 4:15-16).

IV. Christians are members of the Body of Christ:
  A. Relationship to Christ as head—complete subjection.
  B. Relationship to fellow Christians as members—one of complete union and harmony.
   1. Every joint supplying his part makes the body strong (Eph. 4:16).
   2. Many members united in one body (Rom. 12:4-5; 1 Cor. 12:12-20).
   3. Each member his work to perform (1 Cor. 12:14-19).
   4. Each member equally important (1 Cor. 12:21-23).

The New Testament Church

    5. Must be no schism or discord among members (1 Cor. 12:24-25).
    6. Sympathetic interest and mutual care for each other (1 Cor. 12:25-27).
    7. Bound together as one body in Christ by ties of fellowship (1 Cor. 10:17).

V. Importance of Being Members of Body:
    A. The Body made up of the saved (Eph. 5:23).
    B. Called unto peace of Christ in one Body (Col. 3:15).
    C. Cannot be subject to head and united with Christ without being member of Body—compare with physical body.
    D. Reconciled to God in Body (Eph. 2:16).
    E. Fulness of Christ in Body (Eph. 1:3, 23).
    F. Become members of Body by obeying commands of Christ (1 Cor. 12:13; Acts 2:41).

Questions for discussion:
1. What is the Spiritual Body of Christ? _____

2. Who are its members? How do we become such? _____

3. Can a man who is not a member be obedient and subject to Christ? _____

4. How complete is the authority of Christ over His Body? _____

5. What are some of the obligations of its members? _____

6. How many Bodies does Christ have? _____

7. What relationships are emphasized in this picture of the Church? _____

8. How is the Body as a whole to be built up? _____

9. Where is reconciliation made possible? _____

10. Can salvation and spiritual blessings be enjoyed outside of the Body of Christ? _____

LESSON 5
THE TEMPLE OF GOD

I. A Place Where God Meets Those Who Worship Him:
  A. In Old Testament:
    1. In tabernacle (Exod. 25:8-9; Lev. 26:11-12; Deut. 12:5; 16:2-6).
    2. In temple built by Solomon (2 Chron. 7:12-16).
    3. God's name recorded there (Exod. 20:24).
  B. In New Testament (Matt. 18:20; Rev. 2:13; 3:8; Col. 3:17; Acts 15:17; Eph. 3:14-15); God's name recorded in Church.

II. A Spiritual Building in Which the Spirit of God Dwells: (1 Cor. 3:9; 16-17; Eph. 2:19-22).

III. Must Be Built According to God's Plan:
  A. God's plan (1 Chron. 28:10-19; Exod. 25:40; Heb. 8:1-5; 1 Cor. 3:10-15; Psa. 127:1).
  B. God's plan for New Testament Church is found in New Testament scriptures.

IV. Christ and Apostles the Foundation (Isa. 28:16-17; 1 Cor. 3:11; Eph. 2:20).

V. Christians the Stones Builded Together into the Temple of God (Eph. 2:19-22; 1 Pet. 2:5, 6, 9-10).
  A. Unbelievers and disobedient cannot be stones (1 Pet. 2:7-8).
  B. Strength of building depends upon stones being securely cemented and builded together in peace and love (Eph. 2:21-22; 4:1-3, 16).

Questions for discussion:
1. What is God's Temple in the world today? _____

2. Where has God's name been recorded today? _____
_____

The New Testament Church

3. Where must the people of God come today to worship? _____
_____

4. What kind of building is the Temple of God today? _____
_____

5. Who inhabits God's Temple? _____

6. Who are the stones in God's Temple? _____
_____

7. How does one become a stone in the Temple? _____
_____

8. Can one be a stone in God's Temple without being a Christian? _____

9. Can one be a stone in God's Temple without being a member of the Church?

10. Where can the plan of God's Temple be found? _____
_____

11. Is it important that God's plan should be followed in the building of His Temple today? _____
_____

12. Upon what does the strength of the Temple depend? _____
_____
_____

13. Can acceptable sacrifices and worship be offered elsewhere than in the Temple? _____
_____

14. What feature of the Church is emphasized in this figure? _____
_____
_____

LESSON 6
THE VINEYARD OF THE LORD

I. Sowing the Seed (Matt. 13:3-9); Parable of the Sower (Matt. 13:18-23); Parable of Sower Explained:
  A. Church sowing agency today (Phil. 1:4-5; 2:15-16; 1 Thess. 1:8; 1 Tim. 3:15.
  B. Gospel is the seed (Luke 8:11).
  C. Seed must not be mixed (Deut. 22:9); corrupted with doctrines and commandments of men (Matt. 15:8; Col. 2:20, 23).

II. Laborers in Vineyard:
  A. Matt. 21:28-31.
   1. Divine call—"go work"
   2. Divine relationship—"Son"
   3. Divine time—"today"
   4. Divine place—"in my Vineyard"
  B. Matt. 20:1-16.
   1. Hiring more laborers.
   2. Went out early in the morning and all through the day—diligence and zeal.
   3. Why there were eleventh-hour idlers—"because no man hath hired us." Can this be said of us?
  C. Matt. 21:33-46.
   1. God's wrath upon the Jew for abusing His gracious provisions (Matt. 21:41-44).
   2. We must be faithful (1 Cor. 4:1-2; 2 Cor. 4:1-2).

III. The Place of Labor:
  A. In the Vineyard:
   1. Wisdom of God made known through the Church (Eph. 3:10-11).
  B. Glorify God in the Church (Eph. 3:21).

IV. Fruit to be Borne for God (John 15:8; Rom. 7:4).
  A. Rom. 11:20-23. To stand by faith or faithfulness.

B. Matt. 21:18-19. The curse of being unfaithful (John 15:2, 6).
C. How?
1. Brotherly love (John 15:12).
2. Caring for poor (Rom. 15:26-28).
3. Every good work (Col. 1:10).
4. Fruits of Spirit (Gal. 5:16, 22-23).
5. Abiding in Christ (John 15:5-7).
6. Contributing (Phil. 4:15-17).
7. Christian growth (1 Pet. 2:1-2).
8. Hiring laborers into Vineyard (Matt. 20:1-9; John 4:35-38; Luke 10:2).

V. The Reward at the End of the Day (Matt. 20:8; 2 Tim. 4:6-8; 1 Pet. 1:3-5, 9; Rev. 2:10).

Questions for Discussion:
1. Who are laborers in God's Vineyard today (Matt. 21:28)? _____

2. Is there any other field of labor in which we may glorify God? _____
3. How diligent ought we to be in the Lord's Vineyard? _____

4. Why are not many people laboring in the Lord's Vineyard (Matt. 20:7)? _____

5. How may fruit be borne? _____

6. When shall we receive the reward of our labors? _____

7. What is the seed that is to be planted in the Vineyard? _____

8. What if this seed is mixed with human teaching? _____

9. Upon what divine relationship does service in the Vineyard depend (Matt. 21:28-31)? _____

10. What feature of the Church does this figure emphasize? _____

PART TWO
THE ORIGIN OF THE CHURCH

INTRODUCTION—The next three lessons deal with the origin of the Church from the viewpoints of (1) time and (2) authority. That is, when did the Church begin and by whose authority was it built? Whose authority controls it? All need to learn well the answers to these important questions. Particular stress should be given to the distinction to be made between Old and New Testament authority and the purposes Old Testament scriptures serve today in the Church of God.

LESSON 7 _____ THE ORIGIN OF THE CHURCH
LESSON 8 _____ THE AUTHORITY OF THE CHURCH
LESSON 9 _____ USE OF OLD TESTAMENT SCRIPTURES

LESSON 7
THE ORIGIN OF THE CHURCH

INTRODUCTION—The next three lessons deal with the origin of the Church from the viewpoints of (1) time and (2) authority. That is, when did the Church begin and by whose authority was it built? Whose authority controls it? All need to learn well the answers to these important questions. Particular stress should be given to the distinction to be made between Old and New Testament authority and the purposes Old Testament scriptures serve today in the Church of God.

I. The Importance of Knowing When the Church Began:
   A. Matter of identity—to distinguish it from Old Testament agencies and also from religious institutions of modern human origin.
   B. To identify its laws—and to see when the law governing the Church of God went into effect.

II. Church Foreshadowed in Old Testament (Heb. 9:11, 23; 10:1):
   A. The Church then was not in existence in Old Testament days.
   B. Old Testament worthies desired to see its era (1 Pet. 1:10-12).

III. Beginning of Church or Kingdom, Subjects of Prophecy:
   A. Isaiah 2:2-3; Micah 4:1-2. To be established
      1. In last days.
      2. In Jerusalem.
      3. New Testament age is "last days" (Heb. 1:1-2; Acts 2:16-17).
   B. Nebuchadnezzar's dream (Dan. 2:31-35); interpretation of dream (Dan. 2:36-45).
   Four Kingdoms:
      1. Babylonian—Nebuchadnezzar, King, 600 B.C. Kingdom fell in 536 B.C. Represented by head of gold.
      2. Medo-Persian, established by Cyrus, King of Persia, and Darius, King of Media, fell in 330 B.C. Represented by the breasts and arms of silver.
      3. Macedonia—Established by Alexander the Great. Divided among his generals in 323 B. C. Represented by belly and thighs of brass.
      4. Roman, established as world power by Octavius Caesar in 30 B. C. Roman kingdom represented by legs of iron and feet of iron and clay. "In the days of these kings" therefore refers to the time of universal em-

pires, and "smote the image upon its feet" signifies that the event which Daniel foresaw, the establishment of the Kingdom of God, would take place after the beginning of the Roman Empire in A.D. 30 and during its existence.
  5. The New Testament begins its story while the Caesars still ruled the world. "In those days came John the Baptist preaching in the wilderness of Judea, saying, repent ye; for the Kingdom of heaven is at hand" (Matt. 3:1-2). What days? (Luke 3:1-2). "In the Fifteenth year of the reign of Tiberius Caesar" (Luke 3:1).

IV. Church Was Not Established By John:
  A. Preached "at hand" or approaching (Matt. 3:1-2).
  B. John was not in the Kingdom (Matt. 11:11).

V. Church Not Established During the Personal Ministry of Jesus—Yet In The Future:
  A. Mark 1:15—"at hand"—Jesus.
  B. Matt. 10:7—"at hand"—Twelve.
  C. Luke 10:9—"come nigh unto you."
  D. Matt. 6:9-10—disciples taught to pray for it.
  E. Matt. 16:18—Christ promised to build.
  F. Matt. 18:1-3—disciples not yet in it.
  G. Mark 9:1—Christ promises that it will come during that generation.
  H. Luke 22:18; 19:11—disciples yet expecting it (Mark 15:43).
  I. Acts 1:6—had not come at time of ascension.

VI. The Beginning:
  A. (1) Kingdom to begin and law to go forth from Jerusalem (Isa. 2:2-3; Luke 24:47).
     (2) Law went forth on Pentecost from Jerusalem (Acts 2:37-38).
     (3) Pentecost the beginning (Acts 2:1-4; 11:15).
  B. (1) The Kingdom was to come with power (Mark 9:1).
     (2) The power was to come with Holy Spirit (Acts 1:8).
     (3) The Holy Spirit came on Pentecost (Acts 2:1-4).
     (4) Therefore the Kingdom came on Pentecost.
  C. (1) The law was to go forth from Jerusalem (Isa. 2:2-3).
     (2) The apostles commissioned to preach (Matt. 28:18-20; Mark 16:15-16) but instructed to wait in Jerusalem for the Holy Spirit to come and guide them before beginning (Luke 24:49).
     (3) Spirit came on Pentecost and began the preaching of the Gospel. The law of the Kingdom began on Pentecost (Acts 2:31-34, 36-38).

VII. Pentecost Marks the Beginning (Acts 11:15):
  A. The beginning of the Christian Age—The New Covenant (Heb. 8:8; 9:15-17).

B. The beginning of the Church.
C. The beginning of gospel preaching.
D. Beginning of the preaching of the remission of sins (Luke 24:47).

VIII. After Pentecost the Church or Kingdom Always Spoken of as in Existence (Acts 2:47; 5:11; 8:1; 11:22; 13:1; 14:27; Col. 1:13; Rev. 1:9).

Questions for Discussion:

1. Why should one know when the Church began? _____

2. How do you know the Church did not exist during the Old Testament period?

3. Outline the prophecy of Isaiah 2:2-3. See also Micah 4:1-2. _____

4. Show how these predictions were fulfilled in Acts 2. _____

5. Give the leading facts of Daniel 2:31-35, 36-45. _____

6. Give the four kingdoms of Daniel's prophecy, and show how this was fulfilled.

7. How do you know the Kingdom was not set up during the days of John the Baptist or during the personal ministry of Jesus? _____

8. Discuss the markers of the actual beginning of the Kingdom. _____

9. What notable day marks the beginning? _____
10. After this date, how was the "Church" or "Kingdom" spoken of? _____

LESSON 8
THE AUTHORITY OF THE CHURCH

I. **The Source of Authority—God Speaking Through Christ:**
   A. Heb. 1:1-2—New Testament message and messenger contrasted with old.
   B. John 1:17—Moses the lawgiver in Old Testament period—Christ in the New.
   C. Matt. 11:27—God revealed through Christ.
   D. John 5:26-27—Authority given to Christ.
   E. John 17:7-8—Christ's message from God—John 12:49-50.

II. **We Are To Be Governed Today by the Authority of Christ, not Moses and the Prophets:**
   A. Acts 3:19-23; Mark 9:2-8—"Hear ye Him."
   B. Matt. 5:21-22; 5:27-28—"But I say unto you."
   C. 1 Cor. 9:21—"Under law to Christ."

III. **Christ's Authority to Be Executed Through His Apostles:**
   A. Matt. 19:27-28.
   B. Matt. 28:18-20.
   C. Matt. 16:17-19.
   D. John 20:22-23.
   E. 2 Cor. 5:18-20.
   F. 1 John 4:6.

IV. **Apostles to be Guided by Holy Spirit:**
   A. John 14:16-17—To be sent to apostles not to world.
   B. John 14:26—To bring to their remembrance what Christ had taught.
   C. John 16:7-15—To convict the world through the teaching of Christ.
   D. Luke 24:49—To wait in Jerusalem for coming.
   E. Acts 2:1-4, 37—Holy Spirit came and through apostolic preaching did convict women and men.

V. **Preaching of Apostles Confirmed by Miracles (Mark 16:16-18; Heb. 2:1, 4; 1 Cor. 12:28, 31; 13:8-10).** These gifts serve temporary purpose of introducing and confirming New Testament truths.

VI. Completeness of Law Thus Delivered:
  A. Rom. 1:16-17—Gospel of Christ contains the righteousness of God from "faith unto faith."
  B. 2 Pet. 1:2-3—Through knowledge of Christ furnished unto all things that pertain unto life and godliness.
  C. 2 Tim. 3:14-17—Furnished completely unto every good work.
  D. Jude 3—Faith once and for all delivered unto the Saints.
  E. Rev. 22:18-19—Must not add to or take from.

Conclusion: The New Testament scriptures, which contain God's will revealed through Christ and His chosen ambassadors, guided and confirmed in their message by the Holy Spirit, constitute a complete and perfect rule of faith and practice for God's people today—the divine Constitution of the Kingdom of God.

Questions for Discussion:
1. What is the source of all authority? _____
2. Through whom did God reveal His authority? _____
3. Who is to be heard above all and at all times? _____
4. How did Christ contrast his authority with that of the Old Testament law? ____
5. Through whom did Christ execute his authority? (Give quotations.) _____
6. How were the apostles to be guided? _____
7. Why did the Holy Spirit come upon the apostles? _____
8. How did the apostles confirm their preaching? _____
9. What is the completeness of the New Testament? _____
10. What if it were added to or taken from? _____

LESSON 9
USE OF OLD TESTAMENT SCRIPTURES

I. The New Testament—The Sole Rule of Faith and Practice:
  A. Review briefly Lesson VIII (Art. 2, 3 and 6).
  B. The New Testament fulfills and supercedes the Old Testament.

II. Old Testament Scriptures Cannot be Recognized as Authoritative Today:
  A. Old Covenant taken out of the way:
    1. Eph. 2:11-16—Old law destroyed that Gentile and Jew might be brought together in Christ.
    2. Col. 2:14-17—Not to be condemned for not keeping the old law.
    3. Rom. 7:1-6—Made dead to the law that they might be married to Christ.
  B. Christ the mediator of a New Covenant under which we live today (Heb. 8:6-13).
    1. Heb. 7:12—Law changed with Priesthood.
    2. Heb. 7:18-22—Christ, the surety of a better covenant.
    3. Heb. 10:1-10—Imperfections of Old erased by New Covenant.
    4. Heb. 9:15-17—New Covenant made effective after death of Christ.
    5. Gal. 5:1-4—To seek to justify ourselves in anything by Old Covenant is disastrous.

III. How Should Scriptures of Old Testament be Used?
  A. As evidence of divinity of Christ (John 1:45; Acts 2:22-34; Luke 24:44; Acts 10:43; John 5:39).
  B. Exemplifying principles of righteousness (Heb. 12:1-2); witnesses here mentioned had been discussed in Heb. 11.
    1. Faith, example of Abraham.
    2. Patience, example of Job.
    3. Courage, Elijah at Mt. Carmel.
    4. Obedience, the failure of Saul (1 Sam. 15:13-23).
  C. To give us hope (Rom. 15:4; I Kings 8:56; Josh. 23:14).

D. To warn us of consequences of disobedience (Heb. 2:1-4; 10:26-31; 1 Cor. 10:1-13).

CONCLUSION: From Old Testament scriptures we learn two lessons of supreme practical importance to us today:
1. God always rewarded and blessed those who obeyed Him.
2. God condemned and punished those who were disobedient. From a study of these 4,000 years of history in the Old Testament scriptures, we see that God's word is steadfast. We cannot afford to trifle therewith.

Questions for Discussion:
1. What lessons are learned on faith and practice (Lesson VIII, Art. 1, 2, 3, 6)? _____

2. Why is the Old Testament not authoritative today in directing the course of Christians? _____

   a. Why was it abolished? _____

   b. Why is one not condemned for not adhering to its teaching? ____

   c. Through whom was it made dead to Christians? _____
   d. Why was the law changed? _____

   e. When was the change made effective? _____

   f. What of those who seek justification by the law? _____

3. Why should the Old Testament be studied? _____

4. What lessons are learned on obedience and disobedience in the Old Testament? _____

PART THREE
THE MISSION OF THE CHURCH

INTRODUCTION—The next four lessons are given to a discussion and study of the mission of the church. It should be remembered that as a divine institution, the church has a divine mission. It is neither political nor social but altogether spiritual in its design. Its concern is not the entertaining of people but the saving of souls.

The primary mission of the New Testament Church is to "evangelize" the world. The word "evangelism" comes from a Greek word meaning "good news." The "evangelist," therefore, is a proclaimer of good news.

LESSON 10 _____ **EVANGELISM**
LESSON 11 _____ **PERSONAL EVANGELISM**
LESSON 12 _____ **EDIFICATION**
LESSON 13 _____ **MINISTRY TO POOR**

LESSON 10
EVANGELISM

INTRODUCTION—The next four lessons are given to a discussion and study of the mission of the church. It should be remembered that as a divine institution, the church has a divine mission. It is neither political nor social but altogether spiritual in its design. Its concern is not the entertaining of people but the saving of souls.

The primary mission of the New Testament Church is to "evangelize" the world. The word "evangelism" comes from a Greek word meaning "good news." The "evangelist," therefore, is a proclaimer of good news.

I. The Importance of This Work:
    A. First seen in the universal need of salvation.
        1. Rom. 3:9-10—All under sin.
        2. Rom. 3:23—All have sinned and fallen short.
        3. Gal. 3:22—All things under sin.
        4. Eph. 2:1-5—Dead in trespasses and sins.
        5. Eph. 2:12—Having no hope, without God.
    B. The gospel of Christ is God's power to save (Rom. 1:16-17).
        1. 1 Cor. 15:1-4—Corinthians saved by gospel.
        2. Acts 11:14—Words to save Cornelius.
        3. 1 Cor. 4:15—Begotten by the gospel (1 Pet. 1:23).
        4. John 15:3—Cleansed by the words of Christ.
        5. Matt. 13:19; Luke 8:11—Word of God is the Seed of Kingdom.
        6. 2 Cor. 4:3-4—Those to whom gospel is veiled perish.
        7. Eph. 3:6—Partakers of promises of Christ.
        8. Acts 20:32—Able to give inheritance among sanctified.
        9. 2 Tim. 1:10—Life and immortality brought to light.
        10. Rom. 16:25-27—Made known unto obedience of faith.

II. The Church is God's Agency in This Work of Evangelization:
    A. Matt. 20:1-16—The Church compared to householder who goes out to hire laborers into the vineyard.
    B. Acts 13:1-3—The Church the sending agency.

The New Testament Church

C. Matt. 13:3-9—The Church the sowing agency.
D. 1 Tim. 3:14-15—The Church the pillar and ground of truth.
E. Eph. 3:10—Wisdom of God to be made known through church.
F. Eph. 3:21—God to be glorified in the Church throughout all ages.
G. Eph. 4:11-12—Building up body of Christ mission of Church.

III. Local Congregations Were the Medium Through Which This Work of the Church Was Done in New Testament Days. They were the only missionary organizations of the New Testament Church.
A. Churches of Macedonia (2 Cor. 11:8-9).
B. Church at Thessalonica (1 Thess. 1:2-8).
C. Church at Philippi (Phil. 1:3-5; 2:25-30; 4:14-20).
D. Church at Antioch (Acts 13:1-3; 14:27-28).
E. Jerusalem Church (Acts 8:1-6).

IV. The Plan Followed in New Testament Days in Propagating the Gospel:
Acts 1:8—Jerusalem, Judea and Samaria, unto the uttermost parts of the earth.

Questions for Discussion:
1. Define the word "evangelism." _____

2. What is the universal need of everyone? Why? _____

3. What is God's only appointed means to save the world? Give the proof. _____
4. What is God's agency to evangelize the world? _____

5. How is this demonstrated in the parable of the laborers in the Vineyard? ____

6. What is to be the sending agency? _____

7. What is the Church in respect to the support of the truth? _____

8. In what way is the Church the "building up" agency? _____

9. Give some New Testament Churches that were centers of missionary work. _

10. What was the divine order of evangelizing the world (Acts 1:8)?
_____
_____

LESSON 11
PERSONAL EVANGELISM

I. Christian Responsibility Is Personal in Its Nature:
   A. Matt. 25:14-15—Parable of talents: each man made responsible for what he was able to do.
   B. Matt. 25:26-30—Consequence of failure to meet responsibility seen in failure of one talent man.
   C. Rom. 1:14—Paul's sense of responsibility.

II. Means of Fulfilling Our Personal Responsibility:
   A. Teaching and preaching the gospel of Christ to others, both publicly and privately:
      1. Rom. 1:15; Acts 20:20, 24, 27—Paul thus discharged his obligations.
   B. Sending others and holding up their hands in such work:
      1. The example of the Philippians (Phil. 1:3-5; 4:15-16).
      2. Necessity of someone sending (Rom. 10:15).
   A. Influence of righteous lives and faithful service:
      1. Our lives are letters read by others (2 Cor. 3:2-3).
      2. Christian influence compared by Christ to saving power of salt and light of world (Matt. 5:13-16).

III. Some New Testament Examples:
   A. Andrew immediately upon being called by the Savior found his own brother and brought him to Jesus (John 1:40-42).
   B. Philip carried the good news of his discovery of Christ to Nathaniel (John 1:43-51).
   C. Paul became all things to all men; that is, he used every legitimate means and made every sacrifice in order to save others (1 Cor. 9:19-23).

IV. The World is the Field—Our Opportunity for such Work Unlimited (Matt. 13:38; Luke 10:1-2; John 4:35-38).

V. The Successful Soul Winner:

A. The blessedness of it (Dan. 12:3; James 5:19-20).
B. Must be persevering—go at all hours (Matt. 20:1-16).
C. Must have love for souls of men (1 John 4:9; Eph. 5:2).
D. Must be prayerful—example of Christ (Mark 1:85; Luke 6:12).
E. Must know your Bible (2 Tim. 2:15); Be careful what you teach to others (1 Cor. 3:10; 1 Tim. 6:3-5; 1 Tim. 4:16).
F. A purpose. A definite effort to persuade a definite person to accept Christ at a definite time—now.

Questions for Discussion:
1. What of Christian responsibility in evangelism?
    a. To what extent is each one responsible? _____

    b. What if one fails to discharge his responsibility? _____

    c. To what extent should one go to discharge his responsibility? _____

2. Name ways in which one may fulfill his responsibility? _____

    a. Give a notable example. _____
    b. How did Jesus enforce this lesson? _____

3. Name two examples of personal evangelism. _____

4. To what extent did Paul go to reach the lost with the gospel? _____

5. How extensive is the field of labor for Christian evangelism? _____

6. Name some blessings that attend the soul winner. _____

LESSON 12
EDIFICATION

I. In What Respects Are We To Grow as Christians?
  A. In grace and knowledge of the truth (2 Pet. 3:18).
  B. In Christlikeness (Eph. 4:15).
  C. In love, in knowledge, and all discernment (Phil. 1:9).
  D. Quiet, industrious Christian characters (1 Thess. 4:9-12).
  E. As a spiritual house to offer sacrifices (1 Pet. 2:5).
  F. In adding Christian graces and becoming partakers of the divine nature (2 Pet. 1:4-13).
  G. In the Lord and the power of His might by putting on the whole armor of God (Eph. 6:10-18).
  H. In faith and love (2 Thess. 1:3; 1 Thess. 3:12-18).
  I. Ability to resist temptation (Jude 17-23; James 4:7; 2 Pet. 5:8-10).
  J. In ability to serve and sacrifice (Rom. 12:1-2).

II. Requisites of Growth:
  A. Things that hinder:
     1. Wickedness, guile, hypocrisy, envies, evil speakings (1 Pet. 2:1-2).
     2. Dullness of hearing (Heb. 5:11).
     3. Youthful lusts (2 Tim. 2:22).
     4. Foolish and ignorant questions (2 Tim. 2:23; 2 Tim. 1:13).
     5. Love of money (1 Tim. 6:10; 6:17-19).
  B. Things that promote spiritual growth:
     1. Spiritual appetite (1 Pet. 2:2).
     2. Exercise (Heb. 5:13-14; 1 Tim. 4:7-8).
     3. Heeding what we hear (Heb. 2:1-3).
     4. Diligence and active service (1 Tim. 4:13-16).
     5. The right spiritual diet (1 Tim. 4:5-6; 6:3; Tit. 2:1; 2 Tim. 2:14-16, 22-23).
     6. Purity of mind and heart (Tit. 1:11-14).
     7. Prayer and communion with the Lord (Phil. 4:5-7; James 1:2-6; Heb. 7:25; Heb. 4:14-16).

III. Avenues Through Which the Church May Encourage This Growth:
   A. Take thought one for another (Phil. 2:1-4, 19-21).
   B. Exhort each other (Heb. 3:12-14; 10:24-25).
   C. The elders to watch after our souls (Acts 20:28-31; Heb. 13:7-17).
   D. Encourage the fainthearted, support the weak, admonish the disorderly, be longsuffering toward all (1 Thess. 5:12-14).
   E. By its worship services (Heb. 10:25; Eph. 5:19; Col. 8: 15-16).
   F. By its teaching program. "Feed the Church of God" (Acts 20:28; 2 Tim. 2:2; Tit. 2:1-8).

Questions for discussion:
1. Define the word "edify." _____

2. In what and how are Christians to grow? _____

3. Name some essentials of growth. _____

4. Specify some things that prevent growth. _____

5. What things promote development? _____

6. How may the Church encourage growth in grace? _____

7. Name some essentials of growth that are so often omitted in the teaching program of the church. _____

8. Define the word "exhortation." _____

9. Who is charged with special responsibility for watching for souls? _____

10. Which is the most difficult—teaching and convincing, or persuading to action?

LESSON XIII
MINISTRY TO POOR

I. The Lesson as Taught by Christ:
   A. The Good Samaritan (Luke 10:25-37).
   B. Opportunity to do good to one in need (Luke 10:36-37; Gal. 6:10).
   C. Those who should have been first to help, passed him by—the priest and Levite (Luke 10:31-32).
   D. Samaritan, though he was hated and despised by the Jews, had mercy and helped. He loved his neighbor (Luke 10:33-37).

II. The Basis Upon Which Such Work Is to be Done:
   A. Self-consecration (2 Cor. 8:3-5).
   B. Love (2 Cor. 8:8).
      1. Proving our love by our liberality and generosity (2 Cor. 8:24).
      2. Love in deed and truth (1 John 3:17, 18).
   C. Gratitude (1 John 3:16; 2 Cor. 8:9).
   D. Sympathy (1 Cor. 12:25, 26; Gal. 6:2).
   E. To glorify God (2 Cor. 9:12, 15).
   F. To keep our hearts centered on God (1 Tim. 6:17-19).

III. A Part of the Mission of the Early Church:
   A. Rom. 12:13; 15:25-27; 1 Cor. 16:15.
   B. Eph. 4:12—Unto the work of ministering.

IV. The New Testament Plan of Operation in Performing This Ministry:
   A. Individual: Dorcas (Acts 9:36-43).
   B. Congregational (Acts 11:29-30; 2:43-45; 2 Cor. 8:19—"According to ability.") (2 Cor. 8:14—"That there may be equality.")
   C. Congregational cooperation in caring for the needy saints (2 Cor. 8:18-21).
   D. Plan for raising these funds (1 Cor. 16:1-2).
      1. Contributed into common treasury, "Lay by in store."
      2. Regularly: "upon the first day of the week."
      3. Individual: "each one of you."

4. Proportionate: "as you have been prospered."
5. Out of the willingness, purpose, and confidence of the heart (2 Cor. 9:6-11).

Questions for discussion:
1. How did Jesus emphasize caring for the poor? _____

2. How is one to be "neighborly"? _____

3. Name some things that should be the basis of caring for the needy. _____

4. How is love always expressed? _____

5. To succeed in the "ministering to the poor," on whom must our hearts be centered? _____

6. Give references that indicate that the early churches cared for the poor. _____

7. Tell how the early disciples cared for the poor: what was the plan of operation? _____

8. Give some examples of each method. _____

9. What plans were used in financing this work? _____

10. What is wrong in using other plans? _____

PART FOUR
CHURCH MEMBERSHIP

INTRODUCTION—The succeeding five lessons are devoted to the question of "What It Means to Be a Member of the Church." The Church of God does not occupy the place in the hearts of men that it should occupy until they realize that, by staying on the outside of the Church, they rob themselves of life's greatest blessings and of the hope of eternal life. The Church is incomparably greater than all human institutions, sectarian or fraternal.

LESSON 14 _____ THE GRANDEUR AND GLORY OF THE CHURCH
LESSON 15 _____ WHAT MEMBERSHIP MEANS
LESSON 16 _____MEMBERSHIP—ITS RESPONSIBILITIES
LESSON 17 _____ HOW TO BECOME A MEMBER

LESSON 14
THE GRANDEUR AND GLORY OF THE CHURCH

INTRODUCTION—The succeeding five lessons are devoted to the qeustion of "What It Means to Be a Member of the Church." The Church of God does not occupy the place in the hearts of men that it should occupy until they realize that, by staying outside of the Church, they rob themselves of life's greatest blessings and of the hope of eternal life. The Church is incomparably greater than all human institutions, sectarian or fraternal.

I. God Is Its Author: It Is Therefore Divine (Heb. 3:4):
  A. It is God's Temple (1 Cor. 3:16).
  B. His dwelling place (Eph. 2:19-22).
  C. Must be built according to His directions (Heb. 8:1-5).
  D. Jesus the builder (Matt. 16:18-20).
  E. Must take heed how we build (1 Cor. 3:10-15; Psa. 127:1).
  F. God refuses to recognize any but His own (Matt. 15:13).
  G. To wear God's name (Eph. 3:14-16).
  H. It is God's institution (1 Cor. 1:2).

II. Christ Is Its Savior And Head:
  A. Gave himself up for it (Eph. 5:25-27).
  B. Savior of the Body (Eph. 5:23).
  C. Head of the Body, which is the Church (Col. 1:18; Eph. 1:22).
  D. Christ our representative in heaven (Heb. 10:19-25; 1 John 2:1-2).

III. Glorious In Its Mission:
  A. Saving of souls by the preaching of the gospel its design.
    1. The pillar and ground of the truth (1 Tim. 3:14-15).
    2. Sending agency (Rom. 10:11-15; Acts 13:1-3).
    3. Wisdom of God made known through the Church (Eph. 3:10).
    4. God glorified in the Church (Eph. 3:21).

IV. All Spiritual Blessings Are Therein:
   A. The Church is the "fullness of Him that filleth all in all" (Eph. 1:23).
   B. All spiritual Blessings are in Christ (Eph. 1:3). Christ's Body and the Church are one (Eph. 1:22-23; Col. 1:18). Christ and the Church are inseparably united (Eph. 5:28-32). Therefore, through the Church we enjoy every spiritual blessing provided for us in Christ Jesus.
   C. We are reconciled unto God in the Body of Christ, which is the Church (Eph. 2:16; Col. 1:18-20).
   D. We get into Christ and the Church upon the same conditions and by the same process (Gal. 3:26-27; Acts 2:41-47).

Questions for Discussion:
1. Who is the builder of all things? _____
2. Who built the Church? _____
3. Show how God and Christ are inseparable in the Church. _____

4. What is the relation of Christ to the Church? (Christ, as the Head, the Body, the members, etc.) _____

5. What of the glorious mission of the Church? Show that it is God's only missionary society on the earth. _____

6. In whom are all spiritual blessings? _____
7. How then are the blessings enjoyed? _____

8. Where did Christ reconcile Jew and Gentile unto God? _____

9. Prove that one enters Christ and the Church on the same conditions. _____

10. Does one "join the Church"? _____

LESSON 15
WHAT MEMBERSHIP MEANS

I. To Be A Member of the Church of Our Lord Means:
   A. To be a member of the Body of which He is the Head (1 Cor. 12:12, 13, 20, 27; Eph. 1:21-23).
   B. To be a worker in the Lord's vineyard (Matt. 20:1).
   C. To be a living stone in the spiritual temple of God (1 Cor. 3:16; 1 Pet. 2:5).
   D. To be married to Christ (Eph. 5:23, 25, 27; Rom. 7:4).
   E. To be a citizen in Christ's Kingdom (Col. 1:12).
   F. To be a child in God's Family (Gal. 3:26, 27).

II. Membership in the Church of Our Lord Means the Enjoyment of the Rich Provisions of God's Grace for His Children:
   A. Fatherly watch-care and protection (1 Pet. 3:12; 5:6, 7; Phil. 4:5-7; 1 Cor. 10:12-13).
   B. Fatherly provision for all needful things (Matt. 6:33; 2 Cor. 9:6-11; Psa. 84:11).
   C. Fatherly correction and chastisement (Heb. 12:5, 13; Jas. 1:2, 3, 12).
   D. Right of appeal to God as a Father (1 Pet. 3:12; Matt. 6:9).
   E. Fellowship with the Saints (Phil. 2:1-4; 4:14-18; Rom. 12:10).
   F. Hope of an Eternal Inheritance (1 Pet. 1:3-5; Gal. 3:29; Rom. 8:14-17).

III. Membership In the Body of Christ In New Testament Days Meant a Life of Holiness, Sanctification and Justification:
   A. "Washed, sanctified, and justified" (1 Cor. 6:11).
   B. "Called to be saints" (1 Cor. 1:2).
   C. A "holy calling" (Eph. 4:1).
   D. To "depart from unrighteousness" (2 Tim. 2:19).

Questions for Discussion:
1. What does it mean to be a member of the Church? _____
_____

2. Give the meaning of the relationship expressed in Division I of the Lesson. ___

3. Specify some of the rich provisions the Lord has provided for those in the Church. ___

4. Why does the Lord chastise his children? ___

5. What is the fullness of the relationship existing between God and his own? ___

6. What is the condition of all before becoming children of God? ___

7. What kind of life does the New Testament demand of Church members? ___

8. How did Paul speak of the former and latter state of the Corinthians (1 Cor. 6:11)? ___

9. Define the word "saint." ___

10. Are all Christians saints? ___

LESSON 16
MEMBERSHIP—ITS RESPONSIBILITIES

INTRODUCTION—Every relationship in life that is worth while involves responsibility. Membership in the Church of God bestows upon one the highest and holiest privileges and blessings and, therefore, involves the greatest responsibility and most serious obligations. Some of these responsibilities of membership in the Church are:

I. **Local Church Membership:** Since the congregation is the only unit of organization known in the New Testament for carrying forward the work of the Church, it follows that for a Christian to be in full fellowship with the Church, he must be associated with, be a part of, and amenable to a local church. There is no such thing in the New Testament scriptures as "membership at large" in the Church of God.

Paul in his work always associated himself with a congregation of Christians (Acts 9:26-30; 13:1-3; 14:25-28).

II. **Subjection to Elders As a Member of a Congregation:**
  A. Elders to exercise oversight (1 Pet. 5:1-5).
  B. "Obey them that have the rule over you—they watch for your souls" (Heb. 13:17; 1 Tim. 5:17-19).

III. **Joint Participation or Fellowship in the Work of the Local Church:**
  A. "Ready unto every good work" (Tit. 3:1, 2).
  B. "Every joint supplieth" (Eph. 4:16).
  C. "Every tree known by its own fruit" (Luke 6:44).
  D. "Let each man do" (2 Cor. 8:7, 11-15).
  E. "Prove your own work" (Gal. 6:4, 5).

IV. **Preservation of Unity, Peace and Harmony of the Body:**
  A. "No divisions among you" (1 Cor. 1:10).
  B. "No schism—same care one for another" (1 Cor. 12:24, 25).
  C. "Avoid them that cause division among you" (Rom. 16:17-18; 1 Tim. 6:3-4; Tit. 1:10-11; 2 John 9:11).

E. "Endeavoring (making some definite effort) to keep unity of Spirit in the bond of peace" (Eph. 4:1-3).

V. Preserving and Maintaining the Purity of the Church:
   A. Christ died to establish its purity (Eph. 5:25-27).
   B. We must live to maintain it (2 Tim. 2:19-22; 1 Tim. 6:11; 4:12; 5:22; Phil. 1:27).

VI. Fruit to Be Borne; Church Has a Mission to Fill; Souls To Be Saved:
   A. United with Christ that we might bring forth fruit unto God (Rom. 7:4).
   B. Branches that do not bring forth fruit will be cut off (John 15:2).
   C. So shall ye be my disciples (John 15:8).

Questions for Discussion:
1. What does membership in the Church bestow upon one? _____

2. What is God's only unit of organization for work and service? _____

   a. Should not every Christian be amenable to some congregation? _____

   b. How is a "Christian at large" defeating the mission and purpose of the Church? _____

3. Who has the oversight of the congregation? _____
4. To whom shall the membership submit themselves? How? _____

5. To what extent shall each member participate in the work of the Church? ____

6. In respect to peace and unity, what should each one do? _____

7. To what extent should each one strive for unity? _____

8. Christ died to establish "what" concerning the Church? What is the duty of the member with respect thereto? _____

9. What is the mission of Christians, respecting bearing fruit? _____

LESSON 17
SALVATION AND CHURCH MEMBERSHIP

INTRODUCTION—God does the saving. Salvation is the pardon or forgiveness of God—the "blotting out" of our sins. The Church, then, does not do the saving. The question is, "Can one enjoy the salvation that God has provided without being in the Church of God?"

I. The Essentiality and Importance of the Church Are Seen in Christ's Own Attitude Toward It:
 A. "Purchased with His own precious blood" (Acts 20:28; 1 Pet. 1:18-19)
 B. "Gave Himself up for the Church" (Eph. 5:25).
 C. Thus Christ evidenced His attitude toward the essential quality of the church by the price He paid for its existence.
 D. "Let this mind be in you which was also in Christ Jesus" (Phil. 2:5).

II. One Cannot Be "In Christ" Without Being "In the Church":
 A. Christ is the Head, the Church is His Body, Christians are members (Col. 1:18; Eph. 1:21-23; 1 Cor. 12:27). One cannot be joined to the Head without being a member of the Body, which is the Church.
 B. Christ is King, the Church is His Kingdom (1 Tim. 6:15; Col. 1:13). One cannot be a subject of the King without being a citizen of His Kingdom.
 C. Christ is the Bridegroom, the Church is His Bride (Eph. 5:23-32). The two are one. One cannot be related to Christ, therefore, without being equally related to the Church. A child belongs by the same birth to both the family of his father and mother.
 D. To be in Christ is to be in His Body, which is the Church.
  1. In Christ Jesus, made nigh, by blood (Eph. 2:13).
  2. In One Body, reconciled, by cross (Eph. 2:16).
  3. To be in Christ, therefore, is to be in His Body, and to be in His Body is to be in His Church.

III. All Spiritual Blessings Are in Christ Jesus (Eph. 1:3):

A. The Church is the "fullness of Him that filleth all in all" (Eph. 1:23).

IV. To Be a Member of the Church of Christ Means to Have Your Name Enrolled In Heaven (Heb. 12:22, 23).
A. To not have your name enrolled in Heaven means to be eternally lost at the judgment (Rev. 20:15).

V. The Same Process and Conditions That Save From Sin, Makes One a Christian and Adds One to the Church:
A. Faith, baptism, salvation (Mark 16:15, 16).
B. Faith, baptism, puts one into Christ (Gal. 3:26, 27).
C. Faith, baptism, adds one to the Church (Acts 2:41). There is, therefore, no such thing as being saved by one process and then joining the church of your choice by another.

Questions for Discussion:
1. Who alone saves? Does He save out of the Church? _____
2. How did Christ manifest his attitude toward the Church? _____
3. What should be the attitude of the saved toward the Church? _____
4. Show that the same process that makes one a Christian also makes him a member of the Church. _____
   a. Discuss this from the standpoint of the relationship between the head and body, the King and Kingdom, and the Bride and Bridegroom. _____
   b. How are all made nigh and reconciled in Christ? _____
5. Where are all spiritual blessings found? _____
6. Where is the fullness of Christ found? _____
7. In becoming members of the Church, where is one's name enrolled? _____
8. Must one's name be enrolled in heaven to be saved? _____
9. Show that the conditions of salvation, when met, add one to the Church. _____

LESSON 18
HOW TO BECOME A MEMBER

I. The Testimony of Christ:
   A. Must be born again (John 3:3-5).
   B. Must be converted (Matt. 18:1-3).
   C. The Great Commission (Mark 16:15-16; Matt. 28:18-20; Luke 24:44-49).

II. Testimony of the Apostles:
   A. Saved by foolishness of preaching (1 Cor. 1:21).
   B. Must hear in order to believe (Rom. 10:14-17).
   C. Must believe or die in sin (John 8:24; Mark 16:16).
   D. Must repent and be converted (Acts 3:19; Luke 13:3, 5).
   E. By faith baptized into Christ (Gal. 3:26-27).
   F. Purify souls by obedience to truth (1 Pet. 1:22).
   G. Made free from sin by obedience to doctrine (Rom. 6:17, 18).
   H. Must be led by Spirit (Rom. 8:14).
   I. Must be washed, justified, sanctified (1 Cor. 6:11; 1:2).

III. Taught by Figures:
   A. The new birth (John 3:3-5).
      1. Begotten (1 Pet. 1:23; Jas. 1:18; 1 Cor. 4:15).
      2. Born of water and Spirit (John 3:5; Gal. 3:26-27; Acts 2:38-41).
   B. Marriage to Christ (Eph. 5:23-30; Rom. 7:4).
      1. Acquaintanceship (John 6:44, 45).
      2. Love (1 John 4:19).
      3. Ceremony (Gal. 3:26-27).

IV. Exemplified:
   A. Pentecostians (Acts 2):
      1. What they heard: death, burial, resurrection, and exaltation of Christ (Acts 2:22-34).
      2. What they were told to do: believe beyond a doubt, repent and be bap-

tized in the name of Christ (Acts 2:36-38).
  3. What they did: gladly received the word and were baptized (Acts 2:41).
  4. Its consequences: remission of sins and gift of Holy Spirit (Acts 2:38). Added to the Church (Acts 2:41, 47).
 B. Samaritans: Acts 8:12: heard Philip preach Christ, believed, when they believed they were baptized.
 C. The Corinthians: Acts 18:8: heard, believed, and were baptized.
 D. Every conversion in the book of Acts is but a repetition of this same story. The plan was: hear, believe, repent, confess faith in Christ, be baptized into Christ.

CONCLUSION: When men obey the will of God, their sins are pardoned and God recognizes and accepts them as His own children. They are added to the Body of the saved and enjoy the privileges and share the responsibilities of that relationship. There is no such thing taught in God's Word as being saved by one process and joining the Church by another.

Questions for Discussion:

1. Give the testimony of Jesus concerning becoming members of the Church. ___

2. Name the conditions of salvation as announced by the apostles. ___

3. How does one purify his soul? How is he made free from sin? How did Paul state the matter to the Corinthians? ___

4. What does it mean to be led by the Spirit of Christ? ___

5. Give the elements of the new birth. ___

6. Name the requisites of being married to Christ. ___

7. State how these principles were exemplified in the second chapter of Acts. ___

8. Now show how this was manifested by the Samaritans and the Corinthians.

9. Give some other cases in Acts not here mentioned. _____
   _____

10. Now show that the same process that makes one a Christian also makes him a member of the Church. _____
    _____

THE NEW TESTAMENT CHURCH

PART FIVE
CHURCH GOVERNMENT

INTRODUCTION—We undertake a study in the next four lessons of the divine plan for the organization of the Church. The scriptures furnish unto us a plan of church government, as well as a plan of worship and work. To believe in and accept God's Word as divinely inspired and therefore all-sufficient then requires recognition of the completeness and perfection of the organization of the Church. To undertake to improve upon the Church by reorganization, adding to, or failing to respect God's arrangement for it is to express dissatisfaction with God's ways. We should be moved by the spirit of faith to be satisfied with doing God's work in God's way. The Church of God is able to do all that God wants done upon the earth.

LESSON 19 _____ **THE ORGANIZATION OF THE CHURCH**
LESSON 20 _____ **THE ELDERSHIP**
LESSON 21 _____**DEACONS**
LESSON 22 _____**EVANGELISTS**

LESSON 19
THE ORGANIZATION OF THE CHURCH

I. Two Uses of Word "Church" In New Testament:
  A. Universal, comprehensive sense including all saved of the earth (Matt. 16:18; 1 Tim. 3:15; Eph. 1:22, 23). In this sense, the family of God, Body of Christ, Kingdom of God, are the same (see Lessons 1 to 6 on "The Nature of the Church"). No organization in universal sense; knows no authority but Christ and His Word. Whoever does the will of God and obeys the Gospel belongs to it (Acts 2:41, 47).
  2. Local Churches, limited sense including all God's people in one community (1 Cor. 1:2; Rom. 16:16; Acts 14:28; 5:11; 8:1), "In Jerusalem" (Acts 13:1; 15:22), "In Antioch."

II. The Organization of the Local Church:
  A. An established order. "In every Church" (Acts 14:23). "Set in order the things that are lacking" (Tit. 1:5).
  B. An independent self-governing unit, always spoken of as separate units "Churches of Galatia" (Gal. 1:2), "Churches of Judea" (Gal. 1:22). Several independent Churches in one district, but no district organization (1 Cor. 14:38, 40). In this comprehensive injunction, given to a Church, is implied control of its affairs by the Church.
  C. A plurality of elders in every Church. "Ordained elders in every Church" (Acts 14:23). Elders of the Ephesian Church (Acts 20:17).
  D. Deacons. Bishops and deacons of Philippian Church (Phil. 1:1).
  E. Members (Rom. 12:4, 16:1,2; 1 Cor. 12:27). Identification with a local Church was a practice of New Testament days.

III. Local Organization Only Medium Through Which Early Christians worked:
  A. New Testament mentions no other.
  B. Every good work done through local organization (Eph. 3:10).
   1. Missions. Sent out by local church (Acts 13:1-3); reported to local church

(Acts 14:25-28).
2. Charity (Acts 11:29, 30): Funds for poor saints in Judea were placed in hands of elders of Judean Churches to be administered by them.
3. Various scriptural methods may be used in carrying on the work of the local Church, but otheir organizations either within or without, such as ladies' aid societies or young peoples' societies were unknown then and are therefore unscriptural now.

IV. Cooperation of Local Churches:
  A. Local Churches cooperated in doing their work, but such work was always under the supervision of a local Church and its eldership (Rom. 15:25-26; 2 Cor. 8:1-5; Acts 11: 28-30).

Questions for Discussion:
1. Give two senses in which the term "Church" is used in the New Testament. __
2. Is there any universal organization of the Church? __
3. What is the mission of the local Church? __
4. How completely were the local Churches organized? Give the officials. __
5. What is God's medium of working? __
6. Though what medium did the early churches do mission work, care for the poor, and do the work of edification? __
7. Give examples of such work. __
8. What is wrong with the various "aid" societies ? __
9. How may local Churches cooperate in any good work? __
10. Under whose supervision should all work of the Church be done? __

LESSON 20
THE ELDERSHIP

I. The Office: (1 Tim. 3:1).
  A. Uses of word "Elder." Originally the authority seems naturally invested in those who by virtue of greater age and, consequently, experience, were best suited to govern. Later the idea of age became merged with that of dignity and experience.
  1. Word is used as an adjective to denote seniority (Luke 15:25; Mark 8:31).
  2. Referring to Jewish elders of the synagogues (Matt. 16:21; Mark 8:31; Luke 9:22; Acts 4:5).
  3. Denotes certain persons appointed in local Churches to exercise spiritual oversight over its members (Acts 14:23; 20:17; Tit. 1:5).
  4. Elder, in the last sense, is used synonymously with bishop and pastor, referring to the same office and work (Eph. 4:11). "And . . . he . . . called to him the elders of the church. . . .Take heed unto yourselves and to all the flock, in which the Holy Spirit hath made you bishops, to feed (pastor) the Church. . . ." (Acts 20:17, 28). "For this cause I left thee in Crete, . . . and appoint elders in every city. . . . For the bishop must be blameless as God's steward. . ." (Tit. 1:5-7).
  B. The responsibility and work of an elder.
  1. To feed the Church (Acts 20:28).
  2. Guard the flock from false teachers (Acts 20:29-31).
  3. Ruling the Church (Rom. 12:8; 1 Tim. 5:17).
     a. "Not as Lord's, but as examples" (1 Pet. 5:3).
  4. Tending the flock, "exercising the oversight thereof" (1 Pet. 5:2).
  5. "Watching in behalf of souls" (Heb.18:17).

II. The Qualifications of an Elder:
  A. 1 Tim. 8:2-7. Without reproach, husband of one wife, temperate, sober-minded, orderly, given to hospitality, apt to teach, no brawler, no striker, gentle, not contentious, no lover of money, ruling well his own household, not a novice, of good reputation without.
  B. Tit. 1:6-9. Blameless, husband of one wife, self-control, sober-minded,

given to hospitality, able to exhort and convict the gainsayer, no brawler, no striker, not soon angry, not self-willed, not greedy of filthy lucre, having children that believe, who are not accused of riot or unruly, just, holy, a lover of good.
C. Not self-appointed (Acts 14:23; Tit. 1:5).

III. Our Duty Toward Elders:
A. 1 Tim. 5:17, 18.
B. Not to hear accusations except at mouth of two or three witnesses (1 Tim. 5:19).
C. Obey and respect them (Heb. 13:17).

Questions for Discussion:
1. How was the position of an elder set forth (1 Tim. 3:1)? _____
2. How was the term "elder" originally used? _____
3. Give some examples of its usage. _____
4. What, finally, did the term come to mean? _____
5. Name some of the terms that were used to designate the elders. _____
6. What is the responsibility of the eldership? _____
7. Specify the qualifications of elders. _____
8. Name the traits they are not to possess among their qualifications. _____
9. Point out the positive traits of their qualifications. _____
10. What is the duty of the members toward the elders? _____

LESSON 21
DEACONS

I. The Meaning of the Term:
   A. General. "Deacon" means waiter, attendant, servant, minister. It is derived from the word *diako*, which means to run or hasten. The radical idea of the word "deacon" is active service. In this general sense it includes:
   1. Evangelists (Eph. 6:21; Col. 1:7; 1 Tim. 4:6).
   2. Any and every faithful servant of Christ (John 12:26).
   B. Special. From the association of the word with the office and work of bishops and elders, it is evidenced that the word "deacon" is used also in an official sense.
   1. Phil. 1:1. Here bishops and deacons are distinguished from the saints in general.
   2. 1 Tim. 5:8-18. Association of an especially qualified group with the elders in this passage indicates a regularly constituted or established office.

II. Their Position and Work as Seen From:
   A. The meaning of the word "helper," "minister." In contrast to the word "bishop" which means "overseer," the deacon is a helper or servant of the Church, working as does every other member of the congregation, under the oversight and in assistance to the bishops of the Church.
   B. Acts 6:1-6. From this passage we observe:
   1. These men were selected to relieve the apostles of secular duties and responsibilities in order that they might give themselves more fully to spiritual matters.
   2. These men were selected by the congregation and then appointed by the apostles.
   3. The performance of the work for which they were selected constituted the full measure of special responsibility.

III. Their Qualifications:
   A. 1 Tim. 3:8-13.
   1. Grave.

2. Not double-tongued.
3. Not given to much wine.
4. Not greedy for money.
5. Holding the faith in a pure conscience.
6. Proved.
7. Husband of one wife.
8. Ruling their children and homes well.
  B. Acts 6:1-6.
    1. "A man of honest report," a good reputation both within and without the Church.
    2. "Full of the Holy Spirit," bearing its fruits in his life (Gal. 5:22-24).
    3. "Full of wisdom," a man of prudence and sound judgment.

CONCLUSION. In general, a deacon owes the same service to the Lord and bears the same responsibility as does every Christian. He, however, is one upon whom special responsibility has been laid. The Church, as is true of every institution in the world, needs leaders. Deacons are men upon whom special responsibility can be placed without being shunned or evaded and in whom there can be found to an outstanding degree the qualities of the real Christian character.

Questions for Discussion:
1. Give the general meaning of "deacon." _____
_____
_____
2. To what was the term finally limited? _____
_____
_____
8. How did Paul speak of the Philippian Church (Phil. 1:1)? _____
_____
4. Contrast the meanings of "deacon" and "elder." _____
_____
5. Discuss the work of the deacons in the light of Acts 6:1-6. _____
_____
_____
6. Was their work spiritual or temporal? _____
7. Give the qualifications of deacons. _____
_____
_____
8. Specify the negative qualities they are not to possess. _____
_____

9. Name the positive marks of their qualifications. _____

10. Distinguish between the deacons and other members of the congregation. ___

LESSON 22
EVANGELISTS

I. The Use of the Term; Meaning "A Proclaimer of Good News."
  A. Referring to definite work (Eph. 4:11).
  B. Philip designated an evangelist (Acts 21:8).
  C. Timothy urged to do the work of an evangelist (2 Tim. 4:5).

II The Work of an Evangelist:
  A. The work of Philip. Proclaiming Christ (Acts 8:5, 35). Attended by miracles to confirm the word (Acts 8:6-8; Heb. 2:4). Preached wherever opportunity afforded (Acts 8:40).
  B. Baptizing those who believed (Acts 8:12, 88).
  C. "Reprove, rebuke, exhort" (2 Tim. 4:1-2).
  D. Complete organization of congregations (Tit. 1:5).
  E. Indoctrinate the Church (Tit. 1:13; 2:1, 5).
  F. Perpetuate the gospel by committing it unto others who would faithfully teach it (2 Tim. 2:2).
  G. Give his time fully to the Lord's work (2 Tim. 4:2; 1 Tim. 4:13-16; 2 Tim. 2:4-5).
  H. Warn against dangers of apostasy (1 Tim. 4:1-6).
  I. Protect the Church from false teachers (1 Tim. 1:1-3).
  J. Assist in building up local Churches.
    1. Timothy tarried at Ephesus (1 Tim. 1-3).
    2. Titus was left at Crete (Tit. 1:5).
  K. To summarize, the work of an evangelist was:
    1. Preach the word (2 Tim. 4:2).
    2. Guard the faith (1 Tim. 6:20-21).
    3. "Handle aright the word of truth," that is, apply it to all people and conditions as needed (2 Tim. 2:15) to the end that men might be saved.

III. Qualifications of an Evangelist:
  A. "Keep thyself pure" (1 Tim. 5:22).
  B. "Gentle, apt to teach, forbearing (2 Tim. 2:22-26).
  C. Diligent (2 Tim. 2:15, 16).

D. Steadfast in the faith, loyal in the truth, refusing false speculative doctrines and uncompromising toward those who teach them (1 Tim. 6:3-11; 4:1, 6; 2 Tim. 3:14-17; 4:1-5).
E. An example to them that believe (1 Tim. 4:12).
F. Careful both as to himself and what he teaches (1 Tim. 4:16).

CONCLUSION—Evangelists today—that is, those who undertake to spread the gospel by publicly teaching and preaching it—should strive to fit themselves into these requirements of the New Testament as perfectly as possible. The Word of God is already confirmed and exists now in written form that we might appeal to it for evidence that we are preaching the truth; miracles are no longer needed for that purpose as in New Testament days.

Questions for Discussion:
1. Define the word "evangelist." _____
   _____
2. Give some examples. _____
3. Give the work of an evangelist. _____
   _____
   a. What did Philip do in evangelizing? _____
   b. How did Paul instruct Timothy and Titus?_____
   _____
   c. Give a summary of the work of an evangelist. _____
   _____
4. Name some of the qualifications of an evangelist. _____
   _____
5. How careful should all evangelists be as to conduct?_____
   _____
6. Should the evangelist be under the supervision of the Church of his community?_____
7. Should he be amenable to the eldership of the Church? _____
8. If the evangelist will not identify himself with some Church, does he have any right to expect support from any congregation? _____

PART SIX
UNITY

INTRODUCTION—Five lessons are devoted to the study of the important theme of unity. It is of supreme importance because it is demanded by the Lord. The basis upon which it is to be accomplished has been given and is the only plan or platform that meets God's approval. Division in the religious world at large, or in the congregation, is condemned as contrary to the Spirit and will of our Lord and destructive to the Church and the souls of men. Unity must become the prayer and effort of the individual who would be pleasing unto God.

LESSON 23	IMPORTANCE OF UNITY
LESSON 24	THE UNDENOMINATIONAL CHARACTER OF THE CHURCH
LESSON 25	THE SIN OF DIVISION
LESSON 26	GOD'S PLAN FOR UNITY
LESSON 27	UNITY, AN INDIVIDUAL OBLIGATION

Lesson 23
THE IMPORTANCE OF UNITY

INTRODUCTION—Five lessons are devoted to the study of the important theme of unity. It is of supreme importance because it is demanded by the Lord. The basis upon which it is to be accomplished has been given and is the only plan or platform that meets God's approval. Division in the religious world at large, or in the congregation, is condemned as contrary to the Spirit and will of our Lord and destructive to the Church and the souls of men. Unity must become the prayer and effort of the individual who would be pleasing unto God.

I. Christ Prayed For Unity (John 17:20,21):
   A. The scope of the prayer: "Neither for these (apostles) only do I pray, but for them also that believe on me." All believers are included in its scope.
   B. Its object: "That they may all be one; even as Thou, Father art in me, and I in Thee, that they also may be one in us."
   C. Its ultimate effect: "that the world may believe that Thou didst send me."
   D. Implication: That religious division and denominationalism produce infidelity; and that unity among believers is the effective weapon against infidelity and atheism.
   E. Application: Let no man thank God that there are so many Churches, unless he is thankful that the prayer of Christ has not been answered. Those who respect the will of the Lord should promote UNITY and refuse to foster or further denominationalism or division of any sort among believers in Christ.

II. Unity Demanded at Corinth by Paul (1 Cor. 1:10).
   A. The condition: "For it hath been signified unto me that there are contentions among you" (v. 11). "Now this I mean, that each one of you saith, I am of Paul; and I am of Appollos; and I of Cephas; and I of Christ" (v. 12). Compare this picture with the religious world today.
   B. The demand: "That there be no divisions among you." (1) The Lord recognizes no cause for division as just, except truth. Peace must not be bought at the expense of truth sacrificed or compromised (Matt. 10:34-39).

C. The authority: "Through the name of our Lord Jesus Christ."
D. The method: "That ye all speak the same thing." God's word is the only basis for unity.
E. The fruit: "That ye be perfected together in the same mind and the same judgment."
F. Arguments against sects and divisions:
   1. Division is carnal (1 Cor. 8:1-3).
   2. Division destroys the temple (1 Cor. 8:16-17).
   3. Christ is not divided (1 Cor. 1:16).
   4. Wearing other names while attempting to serve Christ dishonors Him (1 Cor. 1:18,14).
G. Such unity as was demanded of the Corinthians is demanded of us today. Division is still wrong and a dishonor to Christ.

CONCLUSION—From those two passages we conclude (1) that those who foster and promote denominationalism and religious division prevent the fulfillment of the Lord's prayer and (2) are a dishonor to the Lord.

Questions for Discussion:
1. For what did Jesus so earnestly pray? _____

2. What was the extent of the unity for which he prayed? _____

3. Give the implication and application of his prayer for unity. _____

4. What is a common petition included in the prayer of the denominational leaders? _____

5. What did Paul command and exhort the Corinthians? _____

6. What is the force of the word "beseech"? _____

7. Who authorized unity among the believers in Christ? _____

8. How is unity to be secured and maintained? _____

9. Give Paul's argument against sects and divisions. _____
_____
_____

10. How does division make void the Lord's prayer? _____
_____
_____

LESSON 24
THE UNDENOMINATIONAL CHARACTER OF THE CHURCH

I. Undenominational in Scope:
   A. The word "Church" means the "Called Out" (see lesson 1). The Church includes, therefore, all who have been called out into God's service and could not be correctly used in a denominational sense. The word "denomination" suggests a fraction or part of the whole. The Church of God is not a part or fraction of anything.
   B. In scope the Church of God includes all the saved.
      1. God does the adding (Acts 2:41-47).
      2. Those who compose the Church are enrolled in heaven—no mistakes made in this enrollment (Heb. 12:22-28). Whereas the Church of God includes every saved person on earth, there is no denomination that makes such a claim.

II. The Church Universal Always Referred to in Singular:
   A. Matt. 16:18—"My Church."
   B. Matt. 8:2—"The Kingdom of Heaven."
   C. Eph. 1:22-23—"The Church, which is His Body."

III. Its Singular Character Emphasized in Every Bible Picture:
   A. It is called "the Body" (Eph. 1:22,28; Col. 1:18). (See lesson 4.)
      1. One body (Rom. 12:4, 5; 1 Cor. 12:20; Eph. 4:4).
      2. Many members, no schism (1 Cor. 12:20, 25).
      3. One Head, Christ (Eph. 1:21, 23).
   B. "The Kingdom" (Matt. 18:24, 31, 33, 44, 45; Col. 1:18). (See Lesson 3.)
      1. Must be united (Luke 11:17).
      2. Under Christ as King (Luke 23:1, 8; John 18:37).
   B. The Family (Heb. 3:6; Eph. 2:19; 3:15). (See Lesson 2.)
      1. All of God's children are in God's Family.
      2. God has but one Family.
      3. That Family is the Church.

        4. Therefore all of God's children are in the Church.
    C. The "Bride of Christ" (Eph. 5:22, 32). There is but one bridegroom, Christ. There is but one bride, the Church.

IV. To Preserve Its Undenominational Character, the Church Must Have:
    A. No denominational name (1 Cor. 1:12, 15; Col. 3:17; Acts 4:11, 12).
    B. No denominational creed, recognizing no authority but Christ (Matt. 28:18, 20). Under law to Him alone (1 Cor. 9:21; Gal. 6:2).
    C. No denominational organization. Only the local Church with its elders, deacons, and evangelists. The only organization of New Testament days (Phil. 1:1; Acts 14:23; Tit. 1:5).
    D. Uncorrupted worship; following the New Testament plan (Phil. 4:9; Heb. 8:5; John 4:24; 1:17).
    E. No entangling alliances. The Church must not lose her identity in any movement and must remain free from political, economical and secular involvements (Phil. 2:12, 16; 2 Cor. 6:14-18).
    F. No denominational requirements for membership. Asking people to do only what people were told to do in New Testament days (Mark 16:15, 16; Acts 2:41).

CONCLUSION—The only explanation for the existence of denominations in the world today is (1) disregard for Christ's authority and (2) a corruption of God's plan of teaching, work and worship.

Questions to Consider:
1. Define the word "Church." _____

2. Now, show that it is necessarily undenominational. _____

3. Show that the Church includes all the saved. Is this true of any denomination?
_____

4. How is the universal idea of the Church always expressed? _____
_____

5. Name some peculiar characteristics of the Church. _____
_____

6. What things are suggested by the terms: "Body," "Kingdom," "Family of God," and the "bride and bridegroom"?_____
_____

The New Testament Church

7. How may undenominational Christianity be secured? _____
_____
_____

8. Denominations exist today at the expense of what?_____
_____

9. What do denominational leaders disregard?_____
_____

10. How do the denominations corrupt the New Testament?_____
_____

LESSON 25
THE SIN OF DIVISION

I. God Hates Those Who Cause It: Prov. 6:19—"A false witness that uttereth lies, and he that soweth discord among brethren."

II. Factions and Sects Are Classified as Works of the Flesh:
   A. Gal. 5:19, 20—"Now the works of the flesh are manifest, which are these: enmities, strife, jealousies, wraths, factions, divisions, parties."
   B. Rom. 2:8—"But unto them that are factious, and obey not the truth, shall be wrath and indignation."
   C. Jas. 3:13, 18—Jealousy and factions belong to the wisdom that is earthly and are followed by every vile deed.
   D. 2 Pet. 2:1, 2—False teachers with destructive heresies bring swift destruction and cause the way of truth to be evilly spoken of.
   E. 1 Cor. 11:17-18—"Ye come together not for the better but for the worse—for when ye come together in the Church, divisions exist among you."

III. The Church Commanded to "Mark" and "Avoid" Those Who Cause division:
   A. Rom. 16:17, 18—Turn away from them for they serve not our Lord Christ.
   B. 2 John 9-11—To greet and receive such is to partake in his evil works.
   C. Tit. 3:10, 11—First admonish, then refuse.

IV. Division Destroys and Defeats the Church:
   1. Luke 11:17—Divided against itself (as denominationalism would represent the Church) it cannot stand.
   2. Heb. 12:28—The Church of Christ is the Kingdom that cannot be shaken.

V. Unity an Individual Obligation to the Christian:
   A. Eph. 4:3—Give diligence to keep the unity of Spirit.
   B. Phil. 2:3—Doing nothing through faction.

VI. How Division May Be Avoided:
   A. Tit. 2:7—By uncorrupted doctrine and sound speech.
   B. Tit. 1:9—Elders holding to the faithful word, which is according to the teach-

ing; exhorting in sound doctrine and convicting gainsayers.
C. Tit. 3:9, 11—Shunning foolish questions and refusing factious men.
D. 2 Tim. 2:14, 18—By handling the Word of God correctly, refusing to fight about words to no profit, and shunning profane babblings.
E. 2 Tim. 2:23, 25—Refusing foolish and ignorant questions yet dealing in meekness and forbearance with all.
F. 1 Pet. 4:7, 11—By exercising love and hospitality toward each other yet speaking as the oracles of God.
G. 2 Pet. 1:16 to 2:2—By refusing to teach private interpretations of prophecies.
H. 1 Cor. 1:10—By confining ourselves to matters of faith when teaching, thereby all can speak the same thing.

Questions for discussion:
1. What is the attitude of God toward discord? _____
2. Divisions and factions are classified with what catagory of sins? _____
3. How are those who cause division to be dealt with? _____
4. What if they are encouraged in their work (2 John 8-11) ? _____
5. How did Jesus set forth the evil effects of division? _____
6. To what extent is one obligated to keep the unity of the Spirit? _____
7. How will "sound speech" create unity? _____
8. How are "foolish questions" to be handled? _____
9. How will "private interpretations" encourage division? _____
10. How will "speaking the same things" maintain unity? _____

LESSON 26
GOD'S PLAN FOR UNITY

I. "That They Might Be One In Us" (John 17:20, 21). Believers must be united in Christ. Whatever unity might be effected outside of Christ is a failure.

II. "Speak the Same Thing" (1 Cor. 1:10).
    A. God's word is the only basis of unity. Unity on any other basis than truth is a failure.
    B. Recognition of proper authority in religious matters is essential. The teachings of Christ and the apostles is the standard by which the judgment is to be rendered (Gal. 1:6, 10).

III. The Divine Standard of Unity (Eph. 4:4, 6).
    A. One God, unity in worship.
    B. One Lord Jesus Christ, unity in authority.
    C. One faith, unity in message.
    D. One baptism, unity in practice.
    E. One body, unity in organization.
    F. One hope, unity in desire.
    G. One Spirit, unity in life. These seven unities constitute the only basis upon which unity is possible from the human viewpoint, as well as the only basis upon which it would be acceptable from the divine viewpoint.
    H. To these Peter adds one name (Acts 4:11, 12).

IV. Denominational Corruptions of This Plan:
    A. Present day denominationalism illustrates the first corruption. Described by the "spiritual union, organic division" plea. Based and furthered upon pleas such as these: "One Church is as good as another," "They are just different roads leading to the same place," "We are all trying to get to the same place," etc. All of these are deceptive and illogical, and, furthermore, the whole plan is in direct disagreement with God's plan. Make a comparison of this plan with the above.
        1. This plan is based upon the following essentials:

a. One God.
   b. One Christ.
   c. One Spirit.
   d. One hope.
  2. But disrespects other essentials in God's plan, namely:
     a. One faith (not just any faith)
     b. One baptism (not three modes)
     c. One Body (not 200 churches)
  No man has any more right to thus nullify God's plan for unity on faith, baptism, or organization, than to worship more than one God. They are all essential elements of God's plan.
B. Another plan offered by denominations is thus described: "organic union and spiritual division." This plan goes a step further than the one mentioned above and concedes that there should be one Church organization, insisting, however, that freedom of belief and practice should be allowed. This second plan is illustrated by the modern "union revivals." Such revivals within themselves admit that denominational names, creeds, organizations, doctrines, and practices actually prevent the salvation of souls. All of these are temporarily laid aside during the "union revival" in the interest of reaching more people. This should be done permanently and when all such party characteristics are forgotten and the divine platform of unity is adopted God will be pleased and many more souls will be saved by the truth.

Questions for discussion:

1. What was the prayer of Jesus for his people? For all? _____

2. What are all to speak and what is the standard? _____

3. Give the divine plan of unity. Memorize the "seven units." _____

4. How do denominations thwart the divine plan? _____

   a. Give specific examples. _____

   b. In their zeal, what is the basis of unity (what four essentials)? _____

   c. What three essentials are omitted? _____

5. What is wrong with the claim of "organic union and spiritual division"? _____

6. How do "union revivals" show denominationalism is wrong? _____
_____

&. What is always laid aside in "union meetings"? _____
_____

LESSON 27
UNITY, AN INDIVIDUAL OBLIGATION

I. Endeavoring To Keep the Unity of the Spirit In the Bonds of Peace: (Eph. 4:3)—"Endeavor" demands a positive effort upon the part of each Christian to make a definite contribution toward unity. Peace is an essential requisite of Unity. However, it is well to keep in mind that peace is not to be bought by the sacrifice of truth or compromise with sin (Matt. 10:34).

II. The Importance of Unity Is Seen in That Depending Upon It:
  A. An unobstructed plea for unity cannot be made to the denominational world when division exists within the Church. The consistency of our plea for unity, then, depends upon our maintaining unity.
  B. The strength and influence of the Church against false doctrines and sin is destroyed by a lack of peace and unity in the Church.
  C. The successful accomplishment of the mission of the Church depends upon the right measure of cooperation. Division makes cooperation impossible and robs the Church of strength in fulfilling its mission.
  D. Moreover, the acceptability of Christian worship depends upon members of the Church holding the right attitude toward each other.
    1. The power of unity in prayer (Matt. 18:19-20).
    2. The hope of forgiveness (Matt. 6:12, 14-15).
    3. The acceptability of our sacrifice and service depends upon our effort to be at peace with our brethren (Matt. 5:22-26).

III. Things That Destroy Unity in the Church:
  A. Selfishness (Phil. 2:3-5). This attitude means a lack of love for Christ and His cause; a headstrong desire to have our own way; a failure to regard the rights of others.
  B. Speculative and hobbyistic teaching (Tit. 2:7; 3:9-11; 2 Tim. 2:14; 2 Pet. 1:16 to 2:2).
  C. Uncontrolled tongues (Jas. 3:5-12).
  D. Peevishness—being easily provoked—love will not allow such a disposition (1 Cor. 18:5).

IV. Means of Promoting Unity:
  A. Generosity, self-sacrifice, willingness to submit in matters of judgment (Phil. 2:3-5; Rom. 12:3-5, 16:19).
  B. Unity in faith and teaching—"speak the same things" (1 Cor. 1:10).
  C. Be at peace with all men, insofar as possible (Rom. 12:18-21). Refuse to become a party to ill-feeling.
  D. The characteristics of love will enforce unity (1 Cor. 13:4-7).
  E. Genuine love for the Lord and His Church; refusing to allow the Body of Christ to be divided; "Let there be no divisions among you" (1 Cor. 1:10).

CONCLUSION: To preserve and promote Unity—Practice 1 Cor. 1:10:
  1. Speak the same things.
  2. Allow no divisions among you.
  3. Be perfected together in the same mind and judgment.

Questions for Discussion:
1. Define the word "endeavor." What are all Christians to do? _____

2. What is the price sometimes paid for peace? _____

3. How does division "within" hamper the Church's plea for unity? _____

4. How does division hamper cooperation of the members of the Church? _____

5. What must be the attitude of members of the Church toward each other if the worship is to be acceptable? _____

6. Name some things that destroy the unity of the Church. _____

7. How may unity be promoted? _____

8. Give a summary of the lesson. _____

10. What are the three rules of 1 Cor. 1:10 for the promotion and preservation of unity? _____

PART SEVEN
THE IDENTITY OF THE CHURCH

INTRODUCTION—Lessons XXVIII to XXXV deal with the identity of the Church. The Church of Christ is not only singular in the fact of its oneness but also in its distinction and separateness from every human institution on earth. Built by a divine pattern which must not be corrupted, it is not human in any of its characteristics, but stands out from the world and all human organizations in name, worship, doctrine, work, and organization. The adoption of human names, creeds, practices, or organizations will denominationalize the Church and bring upon those participating therein the displeasure of God. It is the obligation of every Christian to maintain and preserve the separate and distinct character of God's Church—not only apart from the institutions of men—but also in protecting the purity of its character from contamination by ungodliness and worldliness.

LESSON 28	**THE IDENTITY OF THE CHURCH**
LESSON 29	**A SCRIPTURAL NAME**
LESSON 30	**SCRIPTURAL WORSHIP**
LESSON 31	**SCRIPTURAL TEACHING**
LESSON 32	**SCRIPTURAL TEACHING**
LESSON 33	**THE PURITY OF THE CHURCH**
LESSON 34	**THE CHURCH AND WORLDLINESS**
LESSON 35	**THE DISCIPLINE OF THE CHURCH**

LESSON 28
THE IDENTITY OF THE CHURCH

INTRODUCTION—Lessons 28 to 35 deal with the identity of the Church. The Church of Christ is not only singular in the fact of its oneness but also in its distinction and separateness from every human institution on earth. Built by a divine pattern which must not be corrupted, it is not human in any of its characteristics, but stands out from the world and all human organizations in name, worship, doctrine, work, and organization. The adoption of human names, creeds, practices, or organizations will denominationalize the Church and bring upon those participating therein the displeasure of God. It is the obligation of every Christian to maintain and preserve the separate and distinct character of God's Church—not only apart from the institutions of men—but also in protecting the purity of its character from contamination by ungodliness and worldliness.

I. "Build According to the Pattern" (Heb. 8:5).
   A. We are workers or builders together with God (1 Cor. 3:8, 9).
   B. We must follow God's plan or pattern revealed through:
      1. Teachings of Christ and apostles (Matt. 28:18, 20). The things received to be our guide (Phil. 4:9).
      2. Examples of churches of New Testament days (1 Thess. 1:6, 9).
   C. God will refuse to recognize houses built by human plans (Matt. 15:13; 7:21-23; Psa. 127:1).

II. Measuring the Church by Human Standards:
   A. Various reasons offered to justify existence of sectarian efforts in religion: "Doing some good," "Good people in it," "Teaches some truth," "Enjoyable association," etc. As much can be said for every fraternal organization and most human institutions in the world.
   B. Such claims for divine recognition are:
      1. Dishonoring to God. Reduces God's ways to the level of human ways (Isa. 55:8, 9).
      2. Disrespectful to His Word. No justification in part of the truth being taught when another part is disrespected.
      3. Deceiving to untaught men, satisfying them with unscriptural efforts, which God will not recognize.

III. The Church Measured By the Divine Standard:
   A. The Word of God the measuring rod (Rev. 11:1). By it the Temple is to be measured. When God's Word is the guide, the House is built upon the rock and will stand (Matt. 7:24-27). Our efforts are to be judged by the Word of God revealed through Christ (John 12:47-49).
   B. Compare the Church to which you belong with the Church described in the New Testament in the following points:
      1. Name. Can you find the name you wear in the New Testament?
      2. Worship. Are you following the doctrines of men (Matt. 15:7-9)?
      3. Doctrine. Do you teach only what Christ and the apostles taught (Gal. 1:6-11)?
      4. Organization. Are you trying to serve Christ through human organizations?
      5. Mission. Is the work of the Church confined to the divine mission?
      6. Character. Does the Church demand purity of life and character?

IV. Losing Divine Recognition:
   A. The Church is God's House or Family—a people for God's own possession (1 Pet. 2:5-9).
   B. Peculiarity and singularity must be maintained in order to be acknowledged and approved by the Lord (Tit. 2:11-14).
   C. As good soldiers, the church must not become entangled in affairs of the world. (2 Tim. 2:4). Church must not be subservient to political, economic, or social purposes.
   D. To corrupt God's plan in any point is to lose identity.
      1. The example of the Ephesian Church (Rev. 2:4, 5). Candlestick to be removed (Rev. 1:20). Candlestick represented the identity of the Church. Divine recognition to be withdrawn.
   E. To not be identified with the Lord and his people is fatal in the last day. "Depart, I never knew you" (Matt. 7:22-23).

CONCLUSION: We must strive lawfully if we would be crowned (2 Tim. 2:5). Let us therefore do God's work in God's own way.

Questions for Discussion:
1. How must the Church be built? _____

2. In identifying the Church, what pattern of teaching, authority, and examples is to be followed? _____

3. Name some fallacious reasons that are offered to justify the existence of denominations. _____

4. Now show how such claims are dishonoring, disrespectful to God's word, and mislead the untaught. _____
_____

5. What is the divine standard of measurement? _____
_____

6. In what things should one compare the Church to which he belongs with the church found in the Bible in order to be certain to find the true Church? _____
_____

7. What is the Church? _____
_____

LESSON 29
A SCRIPTURAL NAME

INTRODUCTION—In order to be built according to the divine pattern, the Church of God upon the earth must be called by a name designated by the God of heaven and found upon the pages of His Word.

I. Why the Names Given by Men Are Wrong:
   A. Divisive in character, given to designate peculiar parties, sectarian in purpose and effect, separating some professed believers from others by peculiar name, thereby antagonistic to spirit of Christ (John 17:20-21).
   B. Condemned in New Testament scriptures (1 Cor. 1:10-16).
   C. Given to honor some person such as "Lutheran," or exalt some ordinance, such as "Baptist" or to designate some peculiar manner of Church government as "Methodist" or "Presbyterian," thus diverting honor belonging only to Christ.
   D. Acts as stumbling block to sinners, confusing, creates impression that God has many Churches and that anything is all right in the name of Christianity and if anything is all right, then nothing is all right.

II. What Is the God-Given Name Worn In New Testament Days?
   A. A new name to be designated by God, given by divine authority (Isa. 62:2):
      1. To be borne by Paul (Acts 9:16).
      2. Not to be given until the Gentiles had seen God's righteousness (Isa. 62:2).
      3. Fulfilled at Antioch of Syria (Acts 11:26).
         a. "Were called"—*Chrematidzo* means to speak as an oracle, to be divinely warned, to be called or named from a divine source. Then it could not have been given in derision.
         b. God's name called upon the Gentiles (Acts 16:17).
   B. Accepted by Paul (Acts 26:28-29).
   C. Glorify God in this name (1 Pet. 4:14-16). A worthy name (Jas. 2:7).
   D. Names applied to the Church in general—The Church of God (1 Cor. 1:2). Churches of Christ (Rom. 16:16). In its different phases it is called:
      1. Kingdom of God (Matt. 13:24, 31, 33, 44, 45, 47).
      2. Body of Christ (Eph. 1:22, 23; Col. 1:18).

3. House of God (1 Tim. 3:15, 16).
 E. Names applied to individual members:
   1. Christians (Acts 11:26).
   2. Saints (Phil. 4:21).
   3. Disciples (Acts 16:1; 20:7).
   3. Brethren (Col. 1:2). These names are individual names and were never in scripture applied to the Church; hence the Church cannot scripturally be called "The Christian Church."

III. Why Only the Name God Has Given Should Be Worn:
 A. The Church is the bride of Christ and should wear His name (2 Cor. 11:2).
 B. The Church is God's Family, should wear His name (1 Tim. 3:15; Eph. 3:14, 15).
 C. Whatever we do must be done in the name of Christ (Col. 3:17).
 D. It is the only name in which unity can exist. Among the manmade names, the plea that one name is as good as another is true, but there is no name as great as the name of Christ (Eph. 1:20, 21; Phil. 2:9, 11).
 E. The plea of all religious leaders.
   Luther—Do not call yourselves Lutherans.
   Wesley—I would to God all party names were forgotten.
   Campbell—Abandon all party names and take the name Christian.
 F. It is the only name by which men can be saved (Acts 4:11, 12).
 G. To the name of Christ every knee must bow (Phil. 2:9, 11).

CONCLUSION: One who wishes to please the Lord must not wear a name unknown to the Word of God or belong to a Church whose name cannot be found in the Bible.

Questions for Discussion:
1. How may the Church be identified by name? _____

2. Give some reasons why the names given by men are sinful. _____

3. How do human names detract from "divine rights"? _____

4. Describe the God-given name as prophesied by Isaiah. _____

5. How and where was this prediction fulfilled? _____

6. Who was to bear Christ's name? _____
_____

7. By whom and what writers was the name endorsed? _____
_____

8. Why should the name "Christian" be worn by the followers of Christ?
_____
_____

9. Give seven reasons for wearing the name Christian. _____
_____
_____

10. Show how the name of Christ is above all names. _____
_____
_____

LESSON 30
SCRIPTURAL WORSHIP

I. The Lord's Day (Rev. 1:10):
    A. What day is it?
        1. The Sabbath? No.
            a. The Sabbath given to Jews because of deliverance from Egypt (Deut. 5:15).
            b. God said it would cease (Hosea 2:11).
            c. Paul said it did cease with the crucifixion of Christ, with the Law nailed to the cross (Col. 2:13-17)
    B. The first day of the week is the Lord's Day.
        1. The day of resurrection (John 20:1, 8; Luke 24:1, 7).
        2. Jesus met with His disciples on this day (John 20:19, 26).
        3. Church established and Spirit came on that day (Acts 2:1-4). Pentecost always came on first day of week (Lev. 23:15).
        4. Churches of New Testament days worshiped on that day (Acts 20:7); they came together to break bread. (1 Cor. 16:1-2) Laid by in common treasury.

II. The Spirit of Their Worship:
    A. Must be in Spirit (John 4:24).
    B. Worship with grace in your hearts (Col. 3:16).
    C. Making melody with our hearts—our hearts must accompany the singing of our voices (Eph. 5:19).
    D. Praying and singing with spirit and understanding (1 Cor. 14:15).
    E. Our hearts must be in our worship (Matt. 15:7, 9).
    F. Corinthians due to division, carnality, and revelry could not worship with the heart; condemned by Paul (1 Cor. 11:17, 34).

III. The Items of Worship According To New Testament Plan:
    A. Lord's Supper on first day; met to observe it (Acts 20:7); received instructions from Christ through Paul to do so (1 Cor. 11:23-26).
    B. Singing (Col. 3:16; Eph. 5:19). This is the only music provided in the New Testament plan.

C. Prayer (Acts 2:42; 1 Tim. 2:1, 8).
4. Fellowship, laying by in store according to prosperity (1 Cor. 16:1, 2; Acts 2:42).

IV. They Continued Steadfastly in This Worship (Acts 2:42):
1. Christians admonished not to neglect assembly of saints (Heb. 10:25).

CONCLUSION: A corruption of this plan of worship by changing the day, spirit, or item of worship furnished by scriptures means the destruction of the identity of the Church as the Church of God.

The consequence of doing so is the loss of divine recognition (2 John 9). "He that goeth onward and abideth not in the teachings of Christ hath not God."

Questions for Discussion:
1. What is the leading day of the New Testament? _____
2. Why was the Sabbath given? How long did it continue? _____
3. Name some outstanding events of the Lord's day. _____
4. How must God be worshiped? _____
5. What is always to be present in every act of worship? _____
6. Name the items of Church worship. _____
7. What was said of the first church (Acts 2:42) ? _____
8. How may the worship be corrupted? _____
9. What if the Sabbath Day is observed? _____
10. What if the worship is characterized by will worship? _____

LESSON 31
SCRIPTURAL TEACHING

INTRODUCTION—In order to maintain its identity with the Church established by Christ, controlled by His authority, described in the New Testament, the Church today must be scriptural in its teaching.

I. Restrictions as to What May Be Taught:
   A. Christ limited his teaching to "words received from the Father" (John 8:26, 28, 38; 17:8).
   B. The Holy Spirit did not speak from Himself (John 16:18).
   C. The apostles spoke only that which had been revealed to them (2 Pet. 1:16-21; Gal. 1:6-12).
   D. The Church today must limit its teaching, therefore, to revelation of Christ through the apostles (2 John 9:11; Rev. 22:18, 19).

II. Teaching of Christ and the Apostles the Sole and All-Sufficient Creed of the New Testament Church:
   A. The righteousness of God completely revealed therein (Rom. 1:16, 17).
   B. Furnishes unto every good work (2 Tim. 8:14, 17).
   C. Contains all truth (John 16:13).
   D. Furnishes unto all things that pertain to life and godliness (2 Pet. 1:3, 4).
   E. The faith once and for all delivered unto the saints (Jude 3).
   F. One faith (Eph. 4:5).
   G. "Speak the same things" (1 Cor. 1:10).

III. Objections to Human Creeds:
   A. Made by men, therefore unreliable.
   B. Do not meet humanity's need, therefore insufficient.
   C. Must continually be revised, therefore imperfect.
   D. No authority behind them, therefore unenforceable.
   E. Disagreement and conflict with each other; therefore cannot all be true.
   F. Conflict with the Word of God, therefore all wrong.

IV. The Identity of the Church Tested by What It Teaches:

A. In becoming a member of the Church to which you belong, were you asked to do something more than people were required to do in New Testament days? Compare your experience with the cases of conversion in the book of Acts. Pentecostians (Acts 2:36, 41); The Eunuch (Acts 8:12, 34, 38); Saul (Acts 9:8; 22:16); Cornelius (Acts 10); Lydia and the jailor (Acts 16:14, 15, 30, 34).

B. Has the Church to which you belong undertaken to excuse you from doing something which it is the will of God for you to do (Matt. 7:21; John 12:48)?

C. In order to find the religious teaching to which you have subscribed, can you simply go to the New Testament or is it necessary to consult some human creed?

D. Are you left free to believe and teach whatever the New Testament says or have you subscribed to the doctrines and commandments of men, private interpretation of scripture or the humanly authorized theology of some Church?

D. Can you depend upon the teachings of the New Testament to learn how to worship and serve in the Church to which you belong?

CONCLUSION: The identity of the Church can as easily be destroyed by corrupting its teaching as it can be by corrupting its worship or wearing an unscriptural name.

Questions for Discussion:

1. What sort of teaching will establish the identity of the Church? _____

2. How did Christ limit His teaching?_____

3. How did the Holy Spirit speak? _____

4. How were the apostles limited in their teaching? What becomes of those who go beyond the teaching?_____

5. Tell of the sufficiency of the Bible._____

6. Point out the weakness of human creeds. _____
   _____

7. What book of the New Testament gives the execution of the plan of salvation? Give some notable cases of conversion from this book. _____
   _____
   _____

8. Harmonize the cases of conversion given. Show how all complied with the same terms. _____
   _____
   _____

9. How may the identity of the Church be destroyed by its teaching? _____
   _____
   _____

10. How does the name of the Church affect its identity? _____
    _____
    _____

LESSON 32
SCRIPTURAL TEACHING

I. Continue Steadfastly in the Apostles' Doctrine (Acts 2:42):
  A. Received from Christ (Gal. 1:11-12; John 17:8).
  B. The Church taught to observe commandments of Christ to apostles (Matt. 28:18-20; Acts 2:42; 1 Cor. 11:23).
  C. These commandments given to guide the Church (Phil. 4:9; 1 Tim. 3:15; 1 Cor. 2:10-16; 4:15-17; Jude 17-21).
  D. To disregard and refuse apostolic teaching is to reject God, Christ, and the Holy Spirit (1 John 4:6; Luke 10:16; 1 Thess. 4:8).
  E. To go beyond is to become disobedient (1 Cor. 4:6; 2 John 9-11).

IL The Attitude of the Church Toward the Doctrines and Commandments of men:
  A. Prove all things (1 Thess. 5:21-22).
  B. In knowledge and all discernment approve the things that are excellent (Phil. 1:9-10).
  C. Hold to the faithful word, speak the things which befit sound doctrine, reprove false teachers (Tit. 1:9; 2:1).
  D. No longer tossed to and fro with every wind of doctrine (Eph. 4:14).
  E. Believe not every spirit, prove them to distinguish between the spirit of truth and the spirit of error (1 John 4:1-6).
  F. Be not carried away by strange teaching, eat at the altar of truth (Heb. 13:9-19).
  G. Take heed not to be spoiled by the traditions of men (Col. 2:8).
  H. Beware lest being carried away with the error of the wicked ye fall (2 Pet. 3:17-18).
  I. Speak only those things received (Acts 4:19-20).

III. The Attitude of the Church Toward False Teachers:
  A. Beware of the leaven of the Pharisees and Sadducees (Matt. 16:7-12).
  B. Cut off the occasion for false apostles and deceitful workers (2 Cor. 11:12-15).
  C. No fellowship and encouragement to be given to those who walk not ac-

cording to apostolic teaching (2 Thess. 8:6, 14-15).
D. A factious man after first and second admonition refuse (Tit. 3:9-11).
E. Mark and turn away from those who cause division contrary to apostolic teaching (Rom. 16:17-18).
F. Receive not false teachers into your house, give them no greeting lest you become partakers in their evil works (2 John 7-11).

IV. The Disaster of Allowing False Doctrines To Be Taught in the Church:
A. "A little leaven leaveneth the whole lump" (Gal. 5:9).
B. The warning of Jesus to the Church at Pergamum (Rev. 2:14-17).
C. The bishops or elders responsible for protecting the Church from the blighting and destructive effects of false doctrines (Acts 20:27-32).

Questions for Discussion:
1. From whom did Paul and all the apostles get their teaching?_____

2. Why were the commandments of Christ given? What would occur if they were disregarded? _____

3. How must the doctrines of men be treated? _____

4. How must the Church act toward factious men?_____

5. How must the Church deal with false teachings? _____

6. To what should the Church hold fast?_____
7. Of what did Christ continually warn his disciples?_____

8. How will false teaching, if tolerated, affect the Church? _____

9. How did John warn the Pergamum Church?_____

10. Who is responsible for protecting the Church against false teachers? _____

LESSON 33
THE PURITY OF THE CHURCH

I. The Church in New Testament Days Was Composed of Individuals Purified From Sin and Unrighteousness:
  A. Christ died to make this possible. "That he might present it to himself a glorious Church, without spot or wrinkle" (Eph. 5:25-27).
  1. Cleansed by His blood (1 John 1:7).
  B. Obedience to the gospel appropriates and applies this cleansing power to the individual (Rom. 6:17-18; Eph. 5:26; 1 Cor. 6:9-11; 1 Pet. 1:22-23).

II. This Relationship Imposes Separation from the World and a Life of Purity and Holiness:
  A. Be separate, touch no unclean thing, perfect holiness (2 Cor. 6:14; 7:1).
  B. Be not conformed to the world (Rom. 12:1, 2).
  C. Sin no longer to have dominion (Rom. 6:12-14).
  D. Must not continue in former practices, but walk as new creatures (Col. 3:1-14).
  E. Pure religion demands, "Keep oneself unspotted from the world" (Jas. 1:27).
  F. Cannot be a friend of God and also of the world (1 John 2:15-17; Jas. 4:4).
  G. Entered into a covenant with God. (1) God's part to "know them that are his," recognize us as His children; (2) Our part to depart from unrighteousness and be a "vessel unto honor" (2 Tim. 2:19-22).
  H. Walk in light, not in darkness. (1) The Church, the light of of the world (Matt. 5:14-16; (2) Eye evil, full of darkness (Matt. 6:22-24); (3) No fellowship with darkness (Eph. 5:7-13); (4) Walk in the light as He is in the light (1 John 1:7).
  I. The primary obligation concerns one's self:
  1. 1 Tim. 5:22—"Keep thyself pure."
  2. Acts 20:28—"Take heed unto yourselves."

III. For the Church to Allow Sin To Go On Uncorrected and Unreproved, Is To Condone and Embrace It and Will Eventually So Corrupt the Church As To Cause It To Lose Divine Recognition:

A. 1 Cor. 5:1-13:
      "A little leaven leaveneth the whole lump."
      "Have no company with a brother who persists in sin."
      "Put away the wicked man from among yourselves."
   B. Saints must not defile their garments, clothed in white linen representing righteousness (Rev. 19:6-8; 3:4-5).
   C. Candlestick representing identity (Rev. 1:20) may be removed unless repentance takes place (Rev. 2:5).

Questions for Discussion:

1. What did Christ's death have to do with the Church? _____

2. How are all cleansed and prepared for service in the Church? _____

3. What is to be the relationship of the Church between the clean and unclean? _____

4. What is the attitude of the Church toward sin? _____

5. What was said of friendship with the world? _____

6. What is the Church to the world? _____

7. How is each one to keep himself? _____

8. What if the Church tolerates sin on the "inside"? _____

9. What will become of the impenitent Church? _____

10. Give an example of the impenitent Church and God's dealings with it. _____

LESSON 34
THE CHURCH AND WORLDLINESS

INTRODUCTION—When the purity of the Church is corrupted, its identity is destroyed. The line of distinction must be kept clear between the Church and the world. By what standard can a Christian today determine what is permissible as Christian recreation and what is worldly, harmful, and therefore wrong? The Bible does not deal with this problem in specific "thou shalt not" statements, but in principles. This lesson proposes a study of these principles. They have application to those things that are not wrong within themselves but are made wrong because of their influence and effect. Apply these principles to your problems concerning pleasure and recreation:

I. Does It Destroy Your Identity As A Christian by Causing You to Be Regarded as of the World (2 Cor. 6:14; 7:1; Rom. 12:1-2)?

II. Is the Practice Questionable in Your Own Mind and Therefore an Offense to Your Own Conscience?
  1. Rom. 14:23—"Whatsoever is not of faith is sin." Must have "full assurance" that it is acceptable before God.
  2. The approval of the conscience does not make anything right which is otherwise wrong. To violate our conscience is to weaken our own resistance against sin.

III. Does It Have a Weakening Influence on Others and Will It Become a Stumbling Block to Them?
  1. Wrong to eat meat sacrificed to idols when it led others to stumble, though apart from this influence, when done with a good conscience and sanctified with prayer it was all right (1 Cor. 10:23-33; 8:7-13).
  2. The seriousness of wielding the wrong influence (Matt. 18:6-7).

IV. Is It Destructive To Your Body (1 Cor. 6:19-20; 10:31)?

V. Does It Conflict With Your Duty as a Christian (Matt. 6:33; 2 Tim. 2:4)?

VI. Does It Cultivate an Inordinate Fleshly Appetite (Col. 2:20-23: Tit. 2:11-13; Col. 3:5-6; 1 Cor. 8:27)?

VII. Does It Bring You Under Weakening Association and Influence (1 Cor. 15:33; 1 Thess. 5:21-22)?

VIII. Does It Bring Upon You an Unequal Yoke and Place You at a disadvantage in Serving the Lord (2 Cor. 6:14-18)?

CONCLUSION: If the above questions, any of them, must be answered in the affirmative when applied to the pleasure and recreation in which one takes part, then the Gospel of Christ demands that we leave that thing off. Put your own life to the test.

Questions for Discussion:
1. How does the impurity of the Church affect its identity? _____
2. What is to be done with our bodies (Rom. 12:1-2)? _____
3. How should one always regard his conscience? _____
   a. What if the things done cannot be of faith? _____
   b. How should one train his conscience? What is the basis of such training? _____
   c. What if the conscience is violated? _____
4. How should each Christian regard his influence? _____
5. What if our indulgences cause others to stumble? _____
6. What if our amusements encourage fleshly appetites? _____
7. How should the Christian handle his environment: control it or be controlled by it? _____
8. What if our association and contacts with others bring us under obligation to the world: If we are weakened by such, what is to be done? _____

LESSON 35
THE DISCIPLINE OF THE CHURCH

INTRODUCTION—The meaning of discipline, according to Webster, is "treatment suited to a disciple, education, training, subjection to rule, the habit of obedience." It is twofold: (1) instructive and (2) corrective.

I. Instructive Discipline. Preventative in Nature:
  A. The work of the bishops or elders:
    1. Feed the flock (Acts 20:28).
    2. Tend the flock (1 Pet. 5:2).
    3. Take the oversight (1 Pet. 5:2).
    4. Rule well by example (1 Tim. 5:17).
    5. Watch for souls (Heb. 13:17).
    6. Must give account (Heb. 13:17).
  B. The attitude of the Church:
    1. Esteem them highly in love (I Them. 5:12-13).
    2. Submit to them (Heb. 13:17).
    3. Obey them (Heb. 13:7).
    4. Count them worthy of honor (1 Tim. 5:17).
    5. Imitate their faith (Heb. 13:7).
       A recognition of these duties will maintain God's order. To reject them results in anarchy and a state of spiritual rebellion in the Church.

III. Corrective Discipline, Chastizing or Penalizing in Its Nature:
  A. Its importance.
    1. The Lord wants a pure Church (Eph. 5:25-27; 2 Cor. 11:2-3).
    2. To harbor sin, disorder, rebellion, wickedness in the Church brings the frowns and displeasure of the Lord on those guilty of doing so. A little leaven leaveneth the whole lump. (1 Cor. 5:6).
    3. Corrective discipline therefore has a twofold purpose:
       a. To save the Church (1 Cor. 5:5).
       b. To save the guilty party (1 Cor. 5:5).
  B. Upon whom to be exercised:
    1. Those who walk disorderly (2 Thess. 8:6). One who persists in sin, rebels against the teaching (1 Cor. 5:11-13).

2. A busybody, troublemaker, one who will not tend to his own business (2 Thess. 2:11-15).
   3. Those who cause division (Rom. 16:17; 2 John 9-10; Tit. 3:10-11).
C. The scriptural course to pursue (Matt. 18:15-18):
   1. Pray for them (1 John 5:16).
   2. Try to convert them (Jas. 5:19-20).
   3. Restore them if possible (Gal. 6:1).
   4. Admonish them (1 Thess. 5:14).
   5. As a last resort, if they will not repent, withdraw from them (2 Thess. 3:6; 1 Cor. 5:4-5-13).
   6. In which case it is the duty of the Church as a whole to support such action (1 Cor. 5:9-13; 2 John 10-11; Matt. 18:17).

Questions for Discussion:
1. Define the word "discipline." _____
   _____
2. Who are to have the oversight in preventing, if possible, rigid steps in discipline? _____
   _____
3. Name some ways in which they may prevent the exercise of corrective discipline. _____
   _____
4. What is to be the attitude of the Church toward the elders? _____
   _____
5. What does the Lord want the Church to be? _____
   _____
6. Why then is corrective discipline sometimes necessary? _____
   _____
   _____
7. Who are to be disciplined? _____
   _____
8. What course is to be pursued in disciplining the disorderly? _____
   _____
   _____
9. How should the whole Church support the actions of the elders in withdrawal of fellowship? _____
   _____
   _____
10. How are those disciplined to be treated? _____
    _____
    _____

PART EIGHT
THE WORSHIP OF THE CHURCH

INTRODUCTION—Item by item we are to make a special study of the worship of the Church of God. In its worship, as in all other matters, the church must be governed by divine authority. We must worship according to truth if we would worship acceptably. In every item, our practice should be carefully examined to be sure that there is a "thus saith the Lord" for it and that we are not, therefore, exceeding divine authority. "Prove all things, hold fast unto that which is good."

LESSON 36 _____ **THE LORD'S DAY**
LESSON 37 _____ **THE LORD'S SUPPER**
LESSON 38 _____ **MUSIC IN THE WORSHIP**
LESSON 39 _____ **INSTRUMENTAL MUSIC**
LESSON 40 _____ **CHURCH FINANCES**
LESSON 41 _____ **CHURCH FINANCES**
LESSON 42 _____ **CHURCH FINANCES**

LESSON 36
THE LORD'S DAY

INTRODUCTION—The observance of the Lord's Day as a day of worship and service to the Lord is of New Testament origin. In Old Testament days, under the Law of Moses, God's people observed the "Sabbath." It is necessary, therefore, to deal in this lesson with the passing of the Old and the establishment and significance of the New.

I. The Sabbath:
   A. Why it was observed:
      1. Because of Israel's deliverance from bondage (Deut. 5:15).
      2. Given after Jehovah's deliverance of Israel (Deut. 5:8).
      3. It was an institution then only of the Mosaic dispensation and was not observed during the Patriarchy.
   B. By whom observed:
      1. It was a sign between God and Israel (Exod. 31:13-17).
      2. It was not a sign between God and all nations, but was designated as a special sign between God and the Jews.
   C. The Sabbath ended:
      1. Some contend "a perpetual covenant," therefore would not end (Exod. 31:16).
         a. The Sabbath was no more perpetual than incense and animal sacrifice (Exod. 30:8; Num. 28:1-10).
         b. The Sabbath was a perpetual "sign" between God and Israel as His chosen people, but when Israel ended, the Sabbath ended, the end of Israel as a nation (Amos 8:2-10); fulfillment (Matt. 27:45-46; Luke 23:44-45; John 19:30).
      2. The end of the Sabbath prophesied (Hos. 2:11); Fulfilled (Col. 2:14:17).
      3. The covenant with Israel, including the Ten Commandments, has been annulled (Jer. 31:31; Heb. 8:6-9; Rom. 7:1-7; 2 Cor. 3:7-13; Matt. 5:21-22, 27-28).
      4. Those justifying themselves in Sabbath-keeping or anything else by the Law are severed from Christ and fallen from grace (Gal. 5:4).

The New Testament Church

II. The Lord's Day:
A. Its significance:
1. Jesus arose from the dead on the first day of the week: "the first day," "the same day," "the third day," all refer to the same day (Mark 16:9; Luke 24:1, 13, 20-21, 46).
2. Jesus met with the disciples on the first day of the week (John 20:1, 19, 26).
3. The Church established on Pentecost (Acts 2). Pentecost always came on the first day (Lev. 23:15-16).
4. The Holy Spirit came on the first day (Acts 2:1-4).
5. The gospel began to be preached (Acts 2:22-36).
6. Called "the Lord's Day" (Rev. 1:10).

B. Its observance:
1. The New Testament Church assembled for worship (Acts 20:7; 1 Cor. 16:1-2).
2. Breaking of bread, the chief purpose of the first day assembly (Acts 20:7).
   a. This assembly not to be forsaken (Heb. 10:25-26).
   b. "The first day of the week" means every first day just as "remember the Sabbath Day to keep it holy" means every Sabbath Day.
   c. Breaking of bread referred to Lord's Supper (I Cor.10:16-17; Acts 2:42).
3. Observance of the Lord's Day should be in the spirit of the day.
   a. The events taking place on a day determine the spirit of it: Fourth of July, Armistice Day.
   b. Therefore, fishing, picnicking, ball playing, and worldly amusement seeking are not in keeping with the proper observance of the Lord's Day (Rev. 1:10).

Questions for Discussion:
1. When did the observance of the Lord's Day originate? Where is this revealed? _____

2. Why and when was the Sabbath given? _____

3. It was a sign between whom? _____

4. How were the Sabbath, burning of incense, and burnt offerings perpetual? ___

5. When did the Sabbath end? When was it taken out of the way? _____

6. What is the penalty of Sabbath observance (Gal. 5:4)? _____

7. Why is the Lord's Day so significant? _____

8. Upon what day did the early disciples meet? For what purpose? _____

9. How should this day be observed? _____

10. Should every Lord's Day be observed ? _____

LESSON 37
THE LORD'S SUPPER

I. Its Place:
- A. God's House.
  1. Heb. 8:2—A spiritual House.
  2. Heb. 3:1, 6—"Whose House are we."
  3. 1 Tim. 3:15—God's House is the Church.
- B. The table in God's House (Luke 22:29-30); the tabernacle a type (Heb. 9:1-2).
- C. One loaf on the Lord's table (1 Cor. 10:17); one bread, one body, one loaf.
- D. The loaf broken before eating derived title "breaking of bread" (Acts 2:42; Acts 20:7).

II. Its Origin and Authority:
- A. The practice of early Church (Acts 20:7), "came together to break bread."
- B. Taught by the apostles (Matt. 28:18-20); "Teaching them to observe all things whatsoever I have commanded you."
- C. Paul received it from the Lord (1 Cor. 11:23).
- D. Instituted by Christ and delivered unto the apostles (Matt. 26:26-29; Mark 14:22-25: Luke 22:19-20).

III. The Time of Observance:
- A. The primary purpose of the assembly of the Church on the first day of the week (Acts 20:7), "To break bread."
- B. The regularity of the observance (Acts 2:42). "They continued steadfastly in the breaking of bread."
- C. The duty of constant attendance (Heb. 10:25-26). To neglect is to sin willfully.
- D. The first day of the week was a day of regular assembly (1 Cor. 16:1-2).

IV. Its Design:
- A. In remembrance: "In remembrance of me," a memorial of Christ (1 Cor. 11:24-25).
- B. Anticipation, hope, "till I come" (1 Cor. 11:26).
- C. Fellowship (1 Cor. 10:17). "We who are many are one body," a communion.

D. Obedience to the request of Christ made in the very shadow of the cross.
E. To eat regularly and worthily is to maintain spiritual vigor (1 Cor. 11:29-32; John 6:53).

V. Manner of Observance:
A. Must examine self (1 Cor. 11:28). The practice of closed communion wherein men undertake to examine each other is entirely without scriptural authority.
B. Must observe worthily: that is, discerning the Lord's body and the significance of the emblems contained in the supper (1 Cor. 11:27-29).
C. Communion with Christ must be the heart's thought (1 Cor. 10:15-17; 11:29).
D. Must be observed in the peace and harmony of Christian fellowship (1 Cor. 10:17).

Questions for Discussion:
1. Where and why is the supper to be observed? _____

2. Why was it called "supper," and "breaking bread"? _____

3. Who instituted the supper? When? _____

4. From whom did Paul receive his instructions as to the supper? _____

5. When was the supper observed by the early Christians? Give proof. _____

6. Why were the simple elements taken? _____

7. How does regularity in its observance strengthen the saints? _____

8. How should the supper be observed? _____

9. With whom does the participant commune? _____

10. How do you know it should be observed "every" first day of the week? _____

LESSON 38
MUSIC IN THE WORSHIP

INTRODUCTION—Music has its place and purpose in the worship of the Church. This place and purpose have been created by divine authority. In that place and purpose we must recognize the importance of: (1) the kind of music authorized; (2) the purpose music shall serve; and (3) the manner in which it shall be rendered.

I. The Kind of Music Specified:
   A. New Testament scriptures authorize singing only. Matt. 26:30—"When they had sung a hymn they went out." Acts 16:25—"About midnight Paul and Silas were praying and singing hymns unto God."
   Rom. 15:9—"As it is written, therefore will I give praise unto thee among the Gentiles and sing unto thy name."
   1 Cor. 14:15—"I will pray with the spirit and I will pray with the understanding also; I will sing with the spirit, and I will sing with the understanding also."
   Eph. 6:19—"Speaking one to another in psalms and hymns and spiritual songs, singing and making melody with your hearts unto God."
   Col. 3:16—"Let the word of Christ dwell in you richly; in all wisdom teaching and admonishing one another with psalms and hymns and spiritual songs, singing with grace in your hearts unto God."
   Jas. 5:13—"Is any among you suffering? Let him pray. Is any cheerful? Let him sing praise."
   B. The command to sing is specific and excludes all other kinds of music.
      1. God commanded Noah to build the ark of gopher wood—by specifying "gopher," God eliminated all other kinds of wood. (Gen. 6:14).
      2. God's command to Aaron to offer two goats and a ram in atonement sacrifices excluded every other animal (Lev. 16).
      3. God's command to sing excludes any other kind of music. There are only two kinds—vocal and instrumental. God has specified vocal.
      4. When something more is done than "sing," God has been disobeyed (2 John 9-11; 1 Cor. 4:6).
   C. New Testament scriptures are all-sufficient on this point as on all others

pertaining to Christian worship and service (2 Pet. 1:2-3; Rom. 1:17; 1 Cor. 9:21; Matt. 17:5-6; Acts 3:22-23).

III. The Purpose of Singing:
A. Praise and thanksgiving unto God (Heb. 18:15; Acts 16:25; Rom. 15:9; Jas. 5:13).
B. Teaching and admonishing one another (Eph. 5:19; Col. 3:16). Music in Christian worship is to instruct, communicate ideas from one to another, and admonish those engaged in it to right living, in addition to being a medium of praise, thanksgiving and supplication to God.

III. Manner of Rendition:
A. "Unto God"—directed as praise unto God and not for simple entertainment. Whenever music in Christian worship degenerates into an effort to entertain, it becomes a stench in the nostrils of God. We must remember that we are singing to please God—not the multitude (Acts 16:25; Rom. 15:9; Eph. 5:19; Col. 3:16).
   1. When any act of worship is not directed to God, it misses its mark and is therefore vain.
   2. How utterly abominable, then, is the attempt to attract the world by the music of the Church. Let us be primarily concerned with causing God to listen.
B. "In Spirit" (1 Cor. 14:15; Jas. 5:13). "With the heart"—(Eph. 5:19). "With grace in your heart" (Col. 3:16). From this we learn that our hearts must accompany our singing and be thoroughly in accord with the sentiment of the song being sung. In other words, it must be done in all sincerity.
C. "With the understanding"—(1 Cor. 14:15). One can hardly sing sincerely what one does not understand. We need to study the sentiment expressed in the words of our songs and be sure that it is scriptural and that we understand its meaning in order to be able to make that meaning the sentiment of our hearts.
D. So as to be understood. "Speaking one to another" (Eph. 5:19). "Teaching and admonishing" (Col. 3:16). This divine purpose for singing is entirely lost unless the words are scriptural in sentiment and pronounced plainly enough to be understood by the audience. The teaching to be done in singing must be by the words of the song, since the tune or melody cannot teach anyone anything.
E. The kind of songs to be used. "Psalms and hymns and spiritual songs" (Eph. 5:19; Col. 3:16). "Psalms and hymns" appear to have been used interchangeably and not only convey the character in general of the songs to be sung but specify in particular that such compositions are to be "spiritual." Such could scarcely be descriptive of the "Star Spangled Banner," "Yankee Doodle," or "I Washed My Hands This Morning." Neither could any of the light, trivial, jiggy tunes used today be classified as "spiritual."

The New Testament Church

Questions for Discussion:
1. How many kinds of music are there? _____
2. Read and note carefully the quotations on the music as used in the New Testament. _____
3. Is the teaching of the New Testament complete on this matter? _____
4. Specify the purpose of singing. _____
   _____
   _____
5. Is the mission of singing to entertain? Singing is to please whom? _____
   _____
6. Is singing that is acceptably done directed primarily to the listener?
   _____
7. What is the idea expressed in "with the Spirit and understanding"? _____
   _____
   _____
8. What kinds of songs are to be used in the worship? _____
   _____
9. What is wrong with using semi-spiritual songs? _____
   _____
10. Has God specified the kind of music we are to use or has it been left up to our judgment? _____
    _____

LESSON 39
INSTRUMENTAL MUSIC

INTRODUCTION—We have made a special topic for study of this subject in order to examine some of the most commonly used contentions in favor of mechanical instruments being added to the music in Christian worship.

THE ARGUMENT THAT HAS NEVER BEEN MADE:
No one has ever yet contended or argued that instrumental music should be added to the worship because New Testament scriptures, as we have them given to us today by the good providence of God, teach that it should be used.
Not one passage has ever been produced which even indirectly mentions mechanical instruments of music.
Being unable to make this contention, those who use instrumental music have been forced to defend its use upon other grounds. The following arguments are made:

I. It Was Practiced Under the Law of Moses in Old Testament Times:
   A. This same argument would introduce incense, infant church membership, animal sacrifices, polygamy, and everything else that characterized the Old Testament period. "That which proves too much proves nothing."
   B. To practice anything taught by Moses but not taught by Christ is fatal in Christianity, because it places the authority of Moses on a par with the authority of Christ.
      1. To undertake to live under both the Law of Moses and the law of Christ is spiritual adultery (Rom. 7:1-4).
      2. To justify what we do by the Law of Moses is to sever ourselves from Christ and fall from grace (Gal. 5:4).
      3. To go back to the Law of Moses for some practice not taught by Christ and the apostles is to deny the all-sufficiency of New Testament scriptures and disrespect the completeness of Christ's authority (Acts 3:22; Matt. 17:5; Eph. 1:22-23).
      4. To depend upon Old Testament authority for Christian practice is to resurrect an invalid law and deny the effectiveness of Christ's death upon the cross (Col. 2:13-17; Eph. 2:14-16).

5. To depend upon the Old Law is to cling to the shadow and lose the substance (Heb. 10:1).

II. Instrumental Music Is Not Expressly Forbidden in the New Testament:
A. This argument puts a premium on the silence of the scriptures. It creates a respect for what the Bible does not say rather than what it does say. To put it affirmatively it looks like this: one has the right to practice anything that the Bible does not expressly forbid. That leaves the field open for: counting beads in prayer, wearing religious robes, burning incense, praying to the Virgin Mary, changing the Lord's Supper into a common meal, observing the Sabbath, offering animal sacrifices, baptizing babies, dancing, drinking and gambling and many other things that cannot be in any sense justified as a part of Christianity.
B. We must not go beyond what the scriptures teach (2 John 9:11; 1 Cor. 4:6).

III. Instrumental Music Is Only an Aid:
A. It is not just an aid, it is an addition of another kind of music.
B. It is not on a par with books, seats, lights, etc., for when all these have been used, still there has been only singing. But when the instrument is supplied, we have not only singing but singing and playing. An addition has been made.
C. Instrumental music does not aid in carrying out the God-given purpose for music in the worship.
  1. We have no assurance anywhere that it pleases God as praise.
  2. It makes "teaching and admonishing" and "speaking one with another" in singing more difficult by making the words of the song less audible and understandable. It therefore interferes with the divine purpose of singing, rather than aiding it.

IV. A Matter of Christian Liberty:
A. Christian liberty means freedom from the law and the rudiments of the world (Gal. 3:13; 4:3, 10).
B. It is not to be used as an occasion to the flesh (Gal. 5:13).
C. It is not to be exercised in any matter offensive to the conscience of a brother (1 Cor. 10:28-11:1). Instrumental music is offensive to the conscience of many and has always been a source of division.

V. Practiced at Home:
A. Many things morally right but religiously wrong. (1) Washing of hands (Mark 7:3-7;) (2) Washing of feet.
B. Instrumental music is not wrong in itself. If that were true it would be wrong anywhere, but it is wrong to add it to Christian worship when God has not told us to use it.

VI. Expedient. In Order For Anything To Be Expedient From A Scriptural Standpoint, It Must:

A. Be also lawful (1 Cor. 6:12).
B. Must also edify (1 Cor. 10:23).
C. Must not offend conscience of others (1 Cor. 10:28). Instrumental music proves itself inexpedient in all three of these points.

VII. Instrumental Music in Heaven: To grant this does not yet prove that we should have it in the Church, or else we must also have angels, infants, golden bowls of incense, etc.

VIII. *Psallo* the Greek Word From Which We Have the Translation "Sing" in Our English Bibles, Also Means To Accompany the Singing with Instrumental Music.

If this be true, then instrumental music is commanded and is not a matter of choice with those who would obey God. It would be imperative for each one who sings to have his own instrument and do his own playing, since the command is individual and personal in its meaning. Someone else could no more do the playing for a person than they could acceptably sing for him. This becomes ridiculously absurd.

A. Our most reliable translations do not so render the word. American Revised and King James Version, etc.
B. This would make it necessary to go to the Greek language in order to learn how to worship God. Either that or our faith would have to be placed in the word of men about the matter (1 Cor. 2:5).
C. It means that our English Bibles are unreliable and this being true, the truth has not been made accessible to men today.
D. Only the man who believes that God's providence has withheld a knowledge of the truth from men today could so contend.

IX. Final Objections to Instrumental Music:
A. Instrumental music transgresses and disrespects the authority of Christ by injecting something into Christian worship which the Lord and His apostles have not taught (2 John 9-11).
B. Instrumental music corrupts and makes vain our worship in the practice of that which God has not taught (Matt. 15:7-9).
C. It creates dissension and division by being offensive to the conscience of many (1 Cor. 10:28).
D. We cannot worship God in spirit and truth and use it, for it is no part of "all truth" revealed to the apostles by the Holy Spirit (John 16:13; John 4:24).
E. We cannot walk by faith and practice it, for it is not taught in the Word of God, and faith comes by hearing God's Word (Rom. 10:17; 2 Cor. 5:7).
F. It is no part of the divine pattern and we corrupt the plan for God's House and therefore labor in vain when we use it (Heb. 8:1-7; Psa. 127:1).

Questions for Discussion:
1. State the argument that has never been made to defend instrumental music in Christian worship. _____
_____
2. Show the fallacy of going to the Law of Moses to defend its use. _____
_____
3. How does this argument repudiate the authority of Christ? _____
_____
4. State and refute the argument, "It is not expressly forbidden." _____
_____
5. What if we go beyond the things that are written in the New Testament? ____
_____
6. Make and refute the "aid" argument._____
_____
7. Is it on the par with pews, lights, song books, etc.? _____
_____
8. Define Christian liberty and show when it is violated. _____
_____
9. Make and refute the "heaven argument" to justify instrumental music in worship._____
_____
10. Show that the Greek word *psallo* does not justify its use. _____
_____
11. State objections to instrumental music in Christian worship._____
_____

LESSON 40
CHURCH FINANCES

INTRODUCTION—This problem must first be solved with the individual. Money is not inherently bad. Its character depends upon the character of the one who possesses it. The danger is loving, trusting in it, and making the wrong use of it. Wealth by itself does not constitute a vice any more than poverty constitutes a virtue. Allowing money to develop the wrong attitude of heart and failing to consecrate its power to the glory and honor of God is the thing the scriptures condemn and warn against.

I. The Warning Illustrated:
 A. The rich man and Lazarus (Luke 16:19-30). The picture here is that of a man lavishing upon himself all the luxuries his wealth could provide while denying the crumbs from the table to the poor, diseased, helpless beggar at his gate. One who loves what money will buy, so that he refuses the beggar at the gate, cannot be saved.
 B. The rich young ruler (Matt. 19:16-22; Mark 10:7-22; Luke 18-23). Here is a young man who had conquered the appetites of his flesh to the extent of living a clean moral life, but he had not conquered his heart. He loved his possessions more than he loved God. He wanted his money more than eternal life.
 C. The rich fool (Luke 12:13-21). This is the pitiful scene of a man who foolishly thought he could secure his future by heaping together material possessions. He spent his whole life in the task, and when he thought he was secure, he discovered he had made no preparation at all (Psa. 39:6).

II. Warnings in General:
 A. The justice of God does not reward riches (Job 34:19).
 B. Riches cannot provide for the soul (Psa. 49:1-7; Matt. 16:26).
 C. Riches cannot enter eternity (Psa. 49:10, 16-17).
 D. A good name rather to be chosen than great riches (Prov. 22:1).
 E. A grievous evil to keep riches (Eccl. 5:12-15).
 F. Set not your heart on their increase (Psa. 62:10; Matt. 6:19-24).

G. To trust in riches will cause one to fall (Prov. 11:28).
H. Increasing wealth causes one to be "lifted up" (Ezek. 28:1-10).
I. Deceitfulness chokes out Word of God (Matt. 13:22; Mark 4:19; Luke 8:14).
J. Those minded to be rich subject to danger (1 Tim. 6:9-10).
K. The duty of the rich (1 Tim. 6:17-19).
L. The difficulty of rich being saved (Matt. 6:21; Luke 18:24).
M. What rich man was told to do to be saved (Matt. 19:21; Luke 18:22).
N. What rich man did to be saved (Luke 19:1-10).

III. The Remedy:
A. Laying up treasure in heaven (Luke 18:22; Matt. 6:19-24; Luke 12:21-23).
B. Rich in good works (1 Tim. 6:17).
C. Trust in God, not in riches (1 Tim. 6:17).
D. Be faithful as stewards (Luke 16:11).
E. Abound in richness of liberality (2 Cor. 8:2).
F. The example of Moses (Heb. 11:26).
G. Beware of covetousness (Col. 3:5; Luke 12:15; Eph. 5:3; 1 Cor. 6:10).

Questions for Discussion:
1. Show that the character of the possessor of money makes money good or bad. _____

2. Show how the Bible warns against riches; give notable examples.
_____

3. How is a good name compared with riches? _____

4. How long can one retain his possessions? _____

5. Give the quotation on the dangers of those "minded to be rich." _____

6. What did Zacchaeus do to be saved? _____

7. In what should all be rich? _____

8. In what are all to be faithful? _____

9. Tell of the sacrifice of Moses. _____
_____

10. Of what must all beware? _____
_____
_____

LESSON 41
CHURCH FINANCES

INTRODUCTION—The Church of God is engaged in the greatest mission under heaven. Money is an absolute requisite in carrying on the church's work; hence, the proper use of money becomes an important theme in the New Testament and assumes an important place in the Christian's life. The first sin in the Jerusalem Church that we are told of was the sin of Ananias and Sapphira in the matter of giving money to the Lord (Acts 5:1-2). In making money, Christians must take "thought for things honorable in the sight of all men" and use the money they make with the glory of God in mind.

General Principles Governing Church Finances
I. **Stewardship (Luke 16:1-14). Christians Are Stewards. Stewards Are Trustees, Caretakers of That Which Belongs to Another:**
   A. Must be found faithful as good stewards (1 Pet. 4:10; 1 Cor. 4:1-2). Not wasting goods (Luke 16:1).
   B. Must someday render account of stewardship (Rom. 14:12).
   C. Must not hoard for our own security (Luke 12:13-21).
   D. God does not allow us to take out all that we want or feel that we need and give him a little of what is left. He demands a "first fruit offering" (Lev. 23:9-14; Matt. 6:33).
   E. It is then not a question of how much of our substance we are willing to give to the Lord but, on the contrary, the problem is, "How much of what the Lord has entrusted to me shall I keep?"

II. **Fellowship (Acts 2:42) Coordination, Mutual Participation and Effort:**
   A. In love. "Love one another from a pure heart" (1 Pet. 1:22). "Knit together in love" (Col. 2:2).
   B. In suffering. "Bear ye one another's burdens" (Gal. 6:2).
   C. In service (Gal. 2:9-10; Phil. 1:5; 4:16).
   D. In finance. "Let each one of you" (1 Cor. 16:1-2). "According to his ability" (2 Cor. 8:12). "Equality" (2 Cor. 8:13-15). Equality in bearing the financial burden of the Church does not mean one giving as much as another (2 Cor. 10:12) but each one giving according to his ability. Individual ability is the basis of personal responsibility (Matt. 25:41-44). One cannot be in "full

fellowship" until he is doing his part. See the comparison in the story of the widow's mite (Mark 12:41-44).

III. Discipleship (Matt. 16:24).
A. Requires self-sacrifice and giving up the world (Luke 9:57-62; Matt. 19:27-29).
B. Rich young ruler failed here (Matt. 19:16-22).
C. Christ our pattern (Phil. 2:5-8; 2 Cor. 8:9). Measure yourself by this standard and do not be afraid of giving too much.

IV. Love. Consecration of Self the Basis of Giving (2 Cor. 8:1-5; 2 Cor. 8:8; 8:24).
1. Cannot serve both God and mammon (Luke 16:13-15; Matt. 6:19-24).

Questions for Discussion:
1. How important is the mission of the Church? This necessarily involves the use of what? _____

2. What was the sin of Ananias and Sapphira? _____

3. What are Christians in their use of possessions? _____

4. How must each steward handle his Lord's affairs? _____

5. What is the great "question" of stewardship? _____

6. How is Christian fellowship manifested? _____

7. What may be said of "equality"? What does this mean? _____

8. What is the cost of discipleship? _____

9. Who failed to pay the price of such service? _____

10. Who is the Christian's pattern of giving? Of sacrifice? _____

LESSON 42
CHURCH FINANCES

INTRODUCTION—The Lord has presented a plan for financing the work of the Church in New Testament scriptures. As in the case of every other plan God has given, it must be put into operation by faithfulness upon the part of Christians. The obligation is an individual one. We must work the plan and the plan will work.

I. The Individual in God's Plan:
   A. Giving to be an individual matter, "Let each one of you" (1 Cor. 16:1-2).
   B. Individual enterprise to make it possible (1 Thess. 4:11-12; 2 Thess. 3:10-13; Eph. 4:28). The Church is not to enter into some business enterprise in order to be able to finance its work.

II. The Motive in Giving:
   A. A divine command (Matt. 5:42; Luke 6:38).
   B. Helping the poor will obtain the Lord's help (Psa. 41:1-3).
   C. Makes us Godlike (Luke 6:35-38).
   D. It enlarges the heart when sincerely done and purifies it of petty scruples and burdensome follies (Luke 11:38-42).
   E. It lends acceptance to our prayers (Acts 10:1-4).
   F. A means of laying up treasure in heaven (1 Tim. 6:17-19).
   G. It opens for those who practice it the doorway into the bounties of God's grace (Gal. 6:6-10; 2 Cor. 9:6; Luke 6:38).
   H. It is the means of glorifying God (2 Cor. 9:12-15).
   I. It is the way to be happy (Acts 20:35).

III. The Manner of Giving:
   A. The New Testament plan (1 Cor. 16:1-2).
      1. Periodic, "Upon the first day of the week."
      2. Personal, "Let each one of you."
      3. Provident, "Lay by him in store."
      4. Proportionate, "As he may prosper."
      5. Preventive, "That there be no collections when I come."

NOTE: Sometimes it is argued that this is the plan for raising money only for benevolence in the Church. It remains, however, that divine wisdom led Paul to give this plan to Corinth for raising money and good reasoning will convince one that if it will work in raising money for one righteous cause, it will work for another and for all.

B. Other principles governing the matter of giving.
1. Voluntary, the freewill offering of a willing heart and an open hand, "not grudgingly nor of necessity" (2 Cor. 9:7).
2. Purposeful, planned, systematic. "Let each man do according as he hath purposed in his own heart" (2 Cor. 9:7).
NOTE: The Church should have a planned program of work, and every Christian should have a planned program of giving toward making that work possible.
3. Confidently. He who believes God's promises can give liberally without any fear of being caused to suffer by so doing (2 Cor. 9:8-11; Matt. 6:33).

IV. Measure of Giving:
A. Measured by ability "as prospered" (1 Cor. 16:1-2). "Acceptable according to ability" (2 Cor. 8:12).
B. "Bountifully, not sparingly" (2 Cor. 9:6).
C. The grace of liberality (2 Cor. 8:2, 6, 7). Not how little but how much can we give and how great is the need is the principle of liberality (Acts 2:45).

Questions for Discussion:
1. How is the Lord's plan of financing the Church complete? _____
_____
_____
2. What is the individual's responsibility in financing the Lord's work? _____
_____
_____
3. What is everyone to do to execute the Lord's plan? _____
_____
4. Why should all Christians give? _____
_____
5. Give the nine reasons for giving._____
_____
_____
_____
_____
_____
_____

6. How should each one give? _____

7. Analyze the plan of 1 Corinthians 16:1-2. _____

8. How are purposefulness and cheerfulness to characterize one's giving? ____

9. What is the measure of the Christian's giving? _____

10. What is the "grace" of liberality? _____

PART NINE
CHURCHES OF THE NEW TESTAMENT ERA

INTRODUCTION—The remaining lessons in this series have been given to a study of the Churches of the New Testament era. In the first forty-two lessons we have studied the nature, origin, organization, mission, unity, and identity of the Church as set forth in the scriptures. In the remaining ten lessons we see the application of these principles of divine truth concerning the Church to the congregations of the New Testament era. They were commended for their righteousness and reproved for their failures and faults. The historical records given in the New Testament scriptures concerning these various congregations afford us much opportunity to view in practical demonstration the plan and program of Christianity through the Church.

LESSON 43	THE CHURCH AT JERUSALEM
LESSON 44	THE CHURCH AT ANTIOCH
LESSON 45	THE CORINTHIAN CHURCH
LESSON 46	THE CHURCH AT PHILIPPI
LESSON 47	THE CHURCH AT EPHESUS
LESSON 48	THE CHURCH AT THESSALONICA
LESSON 49	THE CHURCH AT ROME
LESSONS 50-52	A STUDY OF THE SEVEN CHURCHES OF ASIA

LESSON 43
THE CHURCH AT JERUSALEM

I. Jerusalem, the First Church:
  A. Jerusalem, the birthplace.
   1. Prophesied by Isaiah (Isa. 2:2-3).
   2. Luke 24:46—"Repentance and remission of sins preached . . . beginning at Jerusalem."
   3. Luke 24:49—"Tarry in the city until clothed with power."
  B. Pentecost the day.
   1. Kingdom to come with power during lives of some then living (Mark 9:1).
   2. Power to come with Holy Spirit (Acts 1:8).
   3. Spirit came on Pentecost (Acts 2:4, 16-17, 83). Therefore, Kingdom came on Pentecost.
  C. Message is preached.
   1. Repentance and remission of sins (Acts 2:38).
  D. Men added to the Church.
   1. 3,000 added in that day (Acts 2:41).
   2. Continued to add daily those who were being saved (Acts 2:47).

II. Jerusalem, the Model Church:
  A. In respectability: "Found favor with all the people" (Acts 2:47). Commanded even the respect of their enemies.
  B. In happiness: "Took their food with gladness and singleness of heart" (Acts 2:46). Gratitude exemplified.
  C. Zeal. "Continuing daily in the temple" (Acts 2:46). Daily teaching the word of God.
  D. In unity.
   1. United in purpose. "With one accord" (Acts 2:46); "Of one heart and soul" (Acts 4:32).
   2. United in prayer. "Lifted up their voices to God with one accord" (Acts 4:24; 12:5-12).
   3. United in sacrifice. "Had all things common" (Acts 2:44). To meet a great need they pooled their assets and dedicated them to the Lord (Acts 4:32-37). Sold and gave into a common treasury to enable the Church to take

care of the need.
    4. United in fellowship. "Continued steadfastly in fellowship" (Acts 2:42).
E. In liberality: stewardship.
    1. Sold and gave according to need (Acts 2:44).
    2. Did not allow anyone to lack (Acts 4:34-35).
    3. None said what he possessed was his own. Stewardship recognized (Acts 4:32).
F. In loyalty.
    1. Continued steadfastly (Acts 2:42).
    2. Triumphantly faithful in persecutions.
        a. By Sadducees (Acts 5:17-39).
        b. By Pharisees (Acts 7:8).
        c. By Jewish State (Acts 12).
G. In growth.
    1. 3,000 added (Acts 2:41).
    2. Number came to about 5,000 (Acts 4:4).
    3. Multitudes of both men and women added (Acts 5:14).
    4. Number of disciples multiplied (Acts 6:7).
H. In organization.
    1. Elders (Acts 15:6; 15:22; 11:29-30).
    2. Deacons (Acts 6).
I. In evangelism.
    1. Went about preaching the word (Acts 8:4).
    2. Sent Peter and John to Samaria (Acts 8:14).
    3. Sent Barnabas unto Antioch (Acts 11:22).

III. How Men Became Members of the Jerusalem Church (Acts 2:36-38; 2:41-47; 3:19; 6:7).

LESSON 44
THE CHURCH AT ANTIOCH

INTRODUCTION—Third largest city in Roman Empire. Controlled commerce of Mesopotamian Plain. Full of mythology. Potent in commerce; powerful in politics; prominent in history. Became the center of missionary activity of the New Testament era.

I. History of the Establishment of the Church at Antioch:
  A. Dispersion of Jerusalem Church (Acts 8:1-4; 11:19).
  B. Preached Jesus in Antioch (Acts 11:20).
  C. They "believed and turned unto the Lord" (Acts 11:21. See Acts 3:19; 2:38).
  D. Jerusalem Church sent Barnabas out to assist (Acts 11:22).
  E. The Church grew as a result of his exhortation (Acts 11:23-24).
  F. Barnabas secured Paul to aid at Antioch (Acts 11:25-26). Continued together for year (Acts 11:26).

II. The Character of the Church:
  A. The name "Christian" first given there (Acts 11:26). Not given to the Church—nowhere called the "Christian Church"—but given to individual disciples (Acts 4:11-12; Col. 3:17; 1 Pet. 4:6).
    1. The Church at Antioch was the first local Church to be composed of both Jews and Gentiles generally (Acts 15:23).
  B. Energetic and zealous in evangelistic work. Two men preached one whole year (Acts 11:24; 15:35).
  C. Well supplied with teachers (evidencing growth and development), making it possible for the Church to reach out into other territory (Acts 13:1-3).
  D. A missionary Church. One of the most prominent in this work. Not only evangelistic at home but missionary abroad. Became the base of Paul, Barnabas, and others' efforts to spread the gospel.
    1. Acts 13:2-3; 14:26-28 — First tour and return to Antioch.
    2. Acts 15:35-36; 18:22-23 — Second tour and return to Antioch.
  E. A benevolent Church. Must have been liberal in giving. Sent relief to Jeru-

salem according to ability. First Church to send relief to those of another locality (Acts 11:29-30).
F. Recognized the local Church as the medium through which to work. "Sending to the elders" (Acts 11:30).
G. Recognized the organization of the New Testament Church and respected the eldership (Acts 11:30; 15:1-2).
H. Recognized the authority of the apostles as final in determining the Truth on controversial questions (Acts 15:1-2).
I. A growing Church. "Much people added to the Lord" (Acts 11:24).
J. They were interested in the study of God's word. This accounted for their strength and growth (Acts 11:26). A year's revival (Acts 15:35).

CONCLUSION—Where could a better example of a Church fulfilling her obligations both at home and abroad be found than at Antioch?

LESSON 45
THE CORINTHIAN CHURCH

I. Its Establishment:
   A. The City. 400,000 population. A center of commerce. Burned in 146 B.C., rebuilt by Caesar in 46 B.C.; colonized with freedmen of the Roman Empire. Citizenship composed of dishonest and licentious people. The character of its people seen in the fact that it contained the Temple of Venus with 1,000 priestesses dedicated to harlotry.
   B. The message preached. The gospel (1 Cor. 15:1-4; 1:18; 2:1-5; 2 Cor. 1:4-6; 1 Cor. 4:15).
   C. The response (Acts 18:8). "Heard, believed, were baptized" (1 Cor. 6:11) "But ye were washed, but ye were sanctified, but ye were justified in the name of the Lord Jesus Christ, and in the spirit of our God."
   D. The means. The establishment of the Corinthian Church was made possible not only by Paul's labors (1 Cor. 9) but also by other churches supporting him (2 Cor. 11:7-9).

II. Its Character:
   A. The virtues of the Corinthian Church.
      1. Complied readily with counsel—were teachable (2 Cor. 7:6-11).
      2. Responsive to opportunity to do good. In benevolent work, readiness and willingness were shown (2 Cor. 8:9-11; 9:1-5).
      3. Loyal to the truth they had learned (2 Cor. 1:24; 7:13-16). (1 Cor. 15:1) "The gospel which I preached unto you . . . wherein ye stand."
         a. Though sin had been committed and wrong had been done, Corinth had not compromised the truth nor forsaken it.
   B. The vices of the Corinthians. Things for which they were reproved.
      1. Division.
         a. Its cause—carnality (1 Cor. 3:1-3).
         b. Its effect—divided body of Christ (1 Cor. 1:18). Destroy the Temple of God (1 Cor. 3:16).
         c. Its cure—speak the same thing; let no division exist; grow together into the same mind and the same judgment (1 Cor. 1:10).

2. Striving about preachers (1 Cor. 3:4-9; 1:13).
3. Sin permitted (1 Cor. 5).
   a. Its danger—Leaven the whole lump in addition to condemning the one guilty (1 Cor. 5:6).
   b. Its cure (1 Cor. 6:3-5). (See Lesson 35 on discipline in the Church.)
4. Brother going to law against brother (1 Cor. 6:1-8).
5. Indifference to conscience of weak (1 Cor. 8:7-18). Personal liberty must not be exercised to the injury of the weak. Christian liberty not to be misused (1 Cor. 10:23-33).
6. Disorder in worship.
   a. At the Lord's Table (1 Cor. 11:17-34).
   b. Confused as to use of gifts. "Let all things be done decently and in order" (1 Cor. 14:33; 14:4).
7. Seeking precedence. Should seek good of whole body (1 Cor. 12:18-31). "Let all things be done unto edifying" (1 Cor. 14:12, 26).
8. Losing identity. Destroying separateness from world (2 Cor. 6:14—7:1).
9. Glorying in men (2 Cor. 10:7). Comparing men with men wrong (2 Cor. 10:12). Should glory only in the Lord. (2 Cor. 10:17-18).

III. Exhortations Delivered to the Corinthians:
   A. "Be ye steadfast, unmoveable, always abounding in the work of the Lord forasmuch as ye know that your labor is not vain in the Lord" (1 Cor. 15:58).
   B. "Watch ye, stand fast in the faith, quit you like men, be strong. Let all that ye do be done in love" (1 Cor. 16:18-14).
   C. "Having therefore these promises, beloved, let us cleanse ourselves from defilement of flesh and spirit, perfecting holiness in the fear of God" (2 Cor. 7:1).
   D. "But as ye abound in everything, in faith, and utterance, and knowledge, and in all earnestness, and in your love to us, see that ye abound in this grace also." (Liberality) (2 Cor. 8:7).
   5. "And herein I give my judgment; for this is expedient for you, who were the first to make a beginning a year ago, not only to do, but also to will. But now complete the doing also; that as there was the readiness to will, so there may be the completion also out of your ability" (2 Cor. 8:10-11).

LESSON 46
THE CHURCH AT PHILIPPI

INTRODUCTION—An important city of Macedonia, commercially, politically, and historically. Philip of Macedonia, Alexander the Great, and great Grecian philosophers made history in this city. Much history of the progress and spread of Christianity centers about the Philippian Church. The first to be planted on the continent of Europe.

I. The Establishment of the Philippian Church:
  A. Events leading up to it.
    1. Paul on second tour (Acts 15:36).
    2. Visits Churches established on first tour (Acts 15:36; 16:5).
    3. Spirit intervenes and prevents Paul from turning aside unto Asia or Bithynia and he journeys to Troas (Acts 16:6-8).
    4. The Macedonian vision and call (Acts 16:9-10). Paul understands that God was directing him to continent of Europe (Acts 16:10).
    5. Goes to Philippi and searches out Jewish place of worship (Acts 16:11-13).
  B. The Philippian Church begins with conversion of Lydia at a prayer meeting of Jewish women (Acts 16:14-15).
    1. Paul preached.
    2. Lydia heard.
    3. Heart opened to give heed.
    4. She was baptized.
  C. The Jailor converted (Acts 16:25-34).
    1. Caused to inquire by earthquake (Acts 16:30).
    2. Paul preached Christ (Acts 16:32).
    3. Jailor believed and was baptized (Acts 16:30-34).
  D. These conversions marked the beginning of the Philippian Church.

II. The Character of This Church:
  A. Such as to make Paul continually thankful to God whenever he thought of them (Phil. 1:3-4).
  B. A liberal Church.

1. Gave liberally to poor (2 Cor. 8:1-5). Philippian Church prominent among these brethren.
   2. Liberal and consistent in their support of Paul (Phil. 4:10-20).
   3. Gave of their own accord (2 Cor. 8:3).
  C. A missionary Church. Extended fellowship to Paul in spreading the gospel (Phil. 1:5).
  D. Steadfast in service. "From first day until now" (Phil. 1:3).
  E. Zealous and diligent. "From first day" (Phil. 1:3). Did not wait until they had a large congregation and fine house paid for to begin to carry the gospel into other territory.
  F. Growing in faith and standing fast. Paul confident of this (Phil. 1:6, 25-30).
  G. Consecrated. "Gave themselves first unto the Lord" (2 Cor. 8:5).
  H. Duly organized. "Bishops and deacons" (Phil. 1:1).
  I. A congregation with strong ties of brotherly love and devotion.
   1. Sent Epaphroditus to Rome to minister unto Paul. "Your messenger and minister unto my need" (Phil. 2:25).
   2. He longed for them and they would receive him upon his return with all joy (Phil. 2:28-29).
   3. Paul's personal attitude toward them (Phil. 4:1; 1:8).
  J. A happy joyful Church. Rejoice and joy the dominant tone of the Philippian epistle.

III. Paul Enjoins:
  A. Paul's prayer for them (Phil. 1:9-11.)
  B. "Let your manner of life be worthy of gospel" (Phil. 1:27-28).
  C. Unity and humility (Phil. 2:1-11).
  D. "Work out your own salvation . . . holding forth the word of life" (Phil. 2:12-16).
  E. "Glory in Christ and have no confidence in flesh" (Phil. 3:3).
  F. Be of the same mind in the Lord (Phil. 4:2).
  G. "In nothing be anxious" (Phil. 4:6). "Think on these things" (Phil. 4:8-9).

LESSON 47
THE CHURCH AT EPHESUS

INTRODUCTION—Three sources of information—Acts of Apostles, book of Ephesians, letters to Churches in Asia (Acts 18:19-21; 19; 20:18-38; Eph. 1 to 6; Rev. 2:1-7).

GENERAL INFORMATION—The city of Ephesus situated in Asia Minor; wealthy, magnificent city; meeting place of oriental religions and Greek culture. Famous temple of Diana here, worshiped by all Asia Minor. Temple one of seven wonders of ancient world.

Paul would have preached here had providence allowed in early stages of second tour (Acts 16:6). At close of journey on way from Corinth to Jerusalem, he stopped at Ephesus, preached in synagogue, and promised to return (Acts 18:19-21). Three years spent in Ephesus on third tour (Acts 20:31; chap. 19). From here Paul wrote the Corinthian Church (1 Cor. 16:8-9). Timothy labored with this Church (1 Tim. 1:3). John spent closing scenes of his life at Ephesus. Aquila, Priscilla, and Apollos were all at Ephesus.

I. The Beginning of the Ephesian Church:
    A. Paul's first visit found Ephesians interested and willing to learn. They besought him to stay (Acts 18:19-21). He did not tarry but promised to return if God was willing.
    B. Apollos is taught the way of the Lord more perfectly by Priscilla and Aquila (Acts 18:24-28).
        1. He was informed about Jesus but misinformed as to subject of baptism, knowing only the baptism of John (Acts 18:25).
    C. Paul returns (Acts 19:1).
        1. Finds disciples who had been baptized with John's baptism (Acts 19:1-3).
        2. Teaches them the difference between John's baptism and baptism in name of Christ (Acts 19:4).
            a. John's baptism conditioned on repentance alone. Baptism commanded by Christ conditioned on both faith in Christ and repentance from sin (Acts 19:4).
            b. John's baptism was not administered in John's name. Men commanded to be baptized in name of Christ (Acts 19:5; 10:47).

3. As a result of this teaching, these disciples were baptized into the name of Christ (Acts 19:5).
  D. Paul's message.
    1. Preached things concerning Kingdom of God (Acts 19:8).
    2. The Word of the Lord (Acts 19:20). The Way (Acts 19:23).
    3 Against images and idolatry—"There are no gods made with hands" (Acts 19:26).
    4. Taught disciples in separate group (Acts 19:9).
    5. Taught anything that was profitable (that which was needed) publicly and from house to house (Acts 20:20).
    6. The Kingdom and the gospel of the grace of God (Acts 20:24-25).
    7. The whole counsel of God (Arts 20:27).
    8. Commended them to God and the word of His grace (Acts 20:32).
  E. The result.
    1. They believed and burned their books of magic and witchcraft (Acts 19:18-20).
    2. They heard the word of truth, trusted and believed (Eph. 1:13).
    3. Saved by the grace of God and through their faith (Eph. 2:8-9).
    4. Were baptized in name of Christ (Acts 19:4-5).
  F. The means enabling Paul to do this missionary work.
    1. Sent out by Church (Rom. 10:15). Must be sent (Acts 13:3). Antioch sent Paul and Barnabas out.
    2. Other churches cooperated in supporting this work (Phil. 1:3-5). This is God's plan.

II. The Character of the Ephesian Church:
  A. A Church of strong conviction as to truth of gospel.
    1. Faith in Christ (Eph. 1:15).
    2. Endured boldness in teaching and preaching the gospel (Acts 19:8).
    3. Tried and proved false teachers (Rev. 2:2, 6).
  B. Diligent in teaching and in studying the truth.
    1. Publicly and from house to house were taught (Acts 20:20).
    2. Heard Paul daily in the school of Tyrannus for two years (Acts 19:9-10). Contrast this with the lack of interest in Bible study conducted weekly in Churches today.
  C. Were not blind followers of the blind.
    1. Investigated and exposed false teachers (Acts 19:13-20; Rev. 2:2).
  D. Did not tolerate sin and evildoers in the Church (Rev. 2:6). Hated work of Nicolaitans (advocates of free love).
  E. Faithful and steadfast, not only in faith, but in works and service (Rev. 2:2).
  F. Endured persecution and hardships for the Lord's sake with patience (Rev. 2:3).
  G. Tender in their devotion and love for Paul (Acts 20:37-38).
  H. A missionary Church. "All Asia heard the Word of the Lord" (Acts 19:10).

Having been taught, they became teachers. The Church, having been planted, established others. Assos, Smyrna, Pergamos, Sardis, Philadelphia, Laodicea, and others grew out of the work done in and around Ephesus. This sort of work is the primary challenge of Christianity.

I. "But, This I have Against Thee" (Rev. 2:4). Their Faults.
   1. "Thou didst leave thy first love." Though formality of service to God had been persistently carried on, they were motivated through fear or by custom and did not have genuine love in their hearts toward God. First love is the love of devotion and espousal. It is characterized by an anxiety to please and serve. It leads one to ask, not "How much must I do?" but, "How much can I do?"
   2. They had held on to the form of godliness but had drifted away from real love and devotion as the motivating power upon which it should rest.
   3. Contrast the Ephesian Church with its "work—labor—patience" (Rev. 2:2) with the "work of faith—labor of love—patience of hope" (1 Thess. 1:3) of the Thessalonian Church.
   4. The indispensability of love as a motive (1 Cor. 13:1-3).
   5. A fatal error unless corrected (Rev. 2:5). The candlestick represented the identity of this congregation as a Church of Christ. To remove the candlestick meant to lose the church's identity (Rev. 1:20). One can, therefore, be outwardly faithful in the performance of his duty and yet lose the spirit of acceptable service in his heart.

III. General Exhortations and Things Enjoined:
   A. To the elders (Acts 20:28-81).
      1. Take heed to yourselves.
      2. Feed the Church.
      3. Protect from false teachers.
   B. Help for the poor and weak (Acts 20:36).
   C. Walk worthily of calling. Chapters 4 and 5 of Ephesian letter.
   D. Take up whole armor of God (Eph. 6).
   E. "Repent and do first works" (Rev. 2:5).

LESSON 48
THE CHURCH AT THESSALONICA

INTRODUCTION—Establishment on second missionary tour (Acts 17:1-9). A great seaport town of Macedonia. Anciently called Therma. Gave its name to bay on which it was situated. The residence of the Roman proconsul who governed the province of Macedonia and of the Questor, who had the care of the emperor's revenues located here. The metropolis of that district, it was the seat of the court of justice. Carried on extensive commerce through its merchants. Remarkable for the number, wealth, and learning of the inhabitants. Paul journeyed to Thessalonica from Philippi.

I. The Establishment of the Church:
  A. Paul, as was his custom, went into the Jewish synagogue. Jews first, the infallible rule in preaching the gospel (Acts 13:44-46).
      1. The reason for this: The Jews were supposed to be prepared by their teaching under the law to receive the gospel. They were already believers in God and did not have to be converted from idolatry. Their fault was prejudice. Through the Jew, God wanted to reach the Gentile. "I have set thee for a light to the Gentiles" (Acts 13:47).
  B. His message—always the same. "This Jesus is the Christ" (Acts 17:3).
      1. Paul had the courage to go into the Jewish synagogue to preach a message contrary to their conception and understanding. He preached boldly and yet gently.
  C. The result. "Some of them were persuaded"—some Jews but more Jewish proselytes accepted the truth. Many prominent women of the town (Acts 17:4).
  D. The means. Paul's own labors (1 Thess. 2:9). Other Churches (Phil. 4-16-16).

II. The Character of the Church:
  A. Possessed a trinity of graces: "work of faith, labor of love, patience of hope." Three great gospel motives and their contribution to the Christian life and character (I Thess. 1:3).
  B. Endured much persecution (I Thess. 1:6, 2:14-16).
  C. An example in influence upon many others (1 Thess. 1:7). "A city set upon a hill" (Matt. 5:14).

D. Missionary: Consistent with the rule in New Testament age, when this Church was established: it recognized its duty to establish others (1 Thess. 1:8).
E. Converted, most of them, from idolatry. Wholehearted conversion to the Lord (1 Thess. 1:9; 2:13).
F. Growing in spiritual strength (2 Thess. 1:3-6).
G. Worthy of Paul's confidence (2 Thess. 3:4).

III. Errors Corrected and Exhortations Given:
A. "Abstain from fornication, possess your own vessel in honor" (1 Thess. 4:1-8).
B. "Study to be quiet and to do your own business . . . that ye may walk becomingly toward them that are without" (1 Thess. 4:11-12).
C. "Work with your hands" (I These. 4:11). "If any will not work, neither let him eat" (2 Thess. 3:10-12).
D. "Withdraw from them that walk disorderly" (2 Thess. 3:6). See Lesson 35 on Church discipline.
E. "Stand fast" (2 Thess. 2:15).
F. Concerning the second coming of Christ: The Thessalonian brethren were much disturbed about false doctrines which had been taught on this subject.
  1. Christ coming to take vengeance on them that know not God and obey not the Gospel (2 Thess. 1:7-8).
  2. Coming for His own. To be caught up in the clouds to meet the Lord in the air and ever be with the Lord (1 Thess. 4:17; Heb. 9:27-28; John 14:1-6).
  3. Before the living who are "in Christ" thus ascend to meet the Lord, the dead "in Christ" shall be raised to ascend with them (1 Thess. 4:15-16).
     a. This does not teach separate resurrections of the righteous dead and the wicked dead, but only that before the living "in Christ" are received by him at his coming, the dead "in Christ" will first be raised and together with the living "in Christ," ascend to meet the Lord. The resurrection of the wicked does not enter into the teaching of the passage at all.
     b. The Bible teaches a general resurrection of the dead when the Lord comes. "All that are in their graves shall hear his voice" (John 5:28-29). "The Lord himself shall descend from heaven with a shout, the voice of archangel, the trump of God" (1 Thess. 4:16).
  4. A personal coming of Christ. "The Lord himself" (1 Thess. 4:16).
  5. Unexpected as thief in night (1 Thess. 5:1-2; 2 Pet. 3:10).
  6. They had been taught that the Lord was about to come—i.e., the time for his coming immediately at hand (2 Thess. 2:1-3). Paul allayed their disturbance with the assurance that the Lord would not taken place until a falling away had come and the man of sin had been revealed (2 Thess. 2:1-2).

7. Paul warns that neglecting to love the truth will result in the belief of error and lead to their condemnation (2 Thess. 2:10-12).
G. Admonished to be respectful toward those who labor among them and are over them in the Lord (1 Thess. 5:12-13).
H. "Admonish the disorderly, encourage the fainthearted, support the weak, be longsuffering toward all" (1 Thess. 5:14).

LESSON 49
THE CHURCH AT ROME

INTRODUCTION—ROME, THE CITY—One of the most celebrated cities in the universe, the capital of Italy, and once of the world, located on the River Tiber. This famous city was founded by Romulus 753 years before the Christian era. Its history is most interesting commercially, architecturally, politically, and religiously. Gibbon spent twenty years and wrote five volumes about Rome. The most important history of Rome, however, took place in a humble dwelling (Acts 28:30-31). Rome, because of its universal power, played an influential part in the complete apostasy of the Church and the formation of the Roman Catholic hierarchy.

THE EPISTLE TO THE ROMANS—The occasion of Paul's writing this epistle can be gathered from the epistle itself. Paul had learned the status of the Christians at Rome from Aquilla and Priscilla (see Rom. 16:3) and probably from other Jews who had also been driven out of Rome by the decree of Claudius (Acts 18:2). Paul found that the Christian in Rome consisted partly of heathens converted to Christianity and partly of Jews who had, with many remaining prejudices, believed in Jesus as the true Messiah. Many contentions arose from claims of the Gentile converts to equal privileges with the Jews and from the absolute refusal of the Jews to admit these claims, unless the Gentile converts became circumcised, so he wrote to adjust and settle these differences.

It is from this letter and other references in other epistles written by Paul from Rome that we obtain the most of our information concerning the Roman Church.

THE ROMAN CHURCH

I. The Origin of the Church:
    A. Obscurity envelops the founding of the Church at Rome. By whom the gospel was actually planted there is not known: it does not appear that any apostle was employed in this work. It was probably carried to Rome by some of those who were converted on the Day of Pentecost in the city of Jerusalem, for there were then at Jerusalem not only devout men, proselytes to the Jewish religion from every nation under heaven (Acts 2:5), but there were strangers from Rome, also (Acts 2:10). It is most reasonable to

believe, especially since we have no evidence of it being otherwise done, that it was by them that Christianity was planted in Rome.
1. Catholicism teaches that Peter established the Church in Rome, but this is disputed by all of the actual evidence in the case.
   a. Peter's own epistles as evidence.
      (1) They were not addressed either to or from Rome.
      (2) Peter did not consider himself the head of the Church anywhere.
         (a) Only a fellow elder on an equal basis with other elders (1 Pet. 5:1).
         (b) Exhorts elders to tend flock without exercising lordship (1 Pet. 5:2).
         (c) Appeals to Paul for confirmation of teaching (2 Pet. 3:15). Was not conscious of having superior authority.
         (d) Taught that all members of the Church constitute a "holy" or "royal priesthood" (1 Pet. 2:5, 9).
   b. Paul's writings disprove Peter's connection with the Church at Rome.
      (1) Wrote epistle to Romans, sending personal salutations to twenty-six people in Rome by name and does not mention Peter.
   c. Luke's writing disproves papal tradition. He records Peter's work in Jerusalem, Samaria, Lydda, Joppa, Caesarea, Antioch, etc., but does not mention Peter going to Rome or having any connection with it. This leaves the doctrine of Peter as bishop of Rome solely as a Catholic tradition without support of any divine evidence at all.
2. Paul did not establish the Church at Rome.
   a. Had desired to go (Acts 19:21).
   b. Had never been to Rome when the epistle was written (Rom. 1:10-13).
   c. Had been hindered from coming (Rom. 15:22).
   d. The Church already in existence when he finally did reach Rome. Brethren from Rome went out some 52 miles to greet him on his arrival (Acts 28:15).

IL The Character of the Church:
   A. Cosmopolitan in character. People gathered from many parts of the world into Rome, as evidenced by Paul knowing so many personally in the Roman Church when he had never been there. See the personal salutations in Rom. 16.
   B. Composed of both Jew and Gentile converts to Christianity, as evidenced by the nature of the Roman Letter. One of Paul's main arguments in the epistle is the equality of the Jew and Gentile in Christ Jesus (Rom. 3:29-30; 10:12).
   C. Disturbed by divisions created contrary to doctrine of Christ (Rom. 16:17-18).
   D. A well-taught Church. Well-indoctrinated with the truth (Rom. 15:14).

E. Jews among membership were considered more favored of God. This is evidenced by Paul's many definite arguments to the effect that God, under the law of Christ, does not recognize the fleshly seed of Abraham because of their being Jews, but accepts as the seed of Abraham all those who walk in the steps of his faith (Rom. 2:28-29; 3:9; 3:21-30; 4:6-9, 11-12, 14-16).
F. Gentiles also among members who considered the Jews to have been rejected, as evidenced by Paul's admonition to them (Rom. 11:1, 13-24).
G. Yet a Church characterized by great faith in God and in Christ (Rom. 16:17-18).
H. Obedient in attitude (Rom. 16:19).

III. The History of the Church:
A. The history of this world-renowned Church is sad because of its prominence and influence in the apostasy that took hold of the Church throughout the world in later centuries. Because of the great influx of Christians into Rome after the death of Claudius when his decree became inactive, and the rapid growth of the Church there, as well as because of its location in the principal city of the world, the Church in Rome exerted a great influence. How great a pity that such an influential Church could not have stood Gibralter-like against the sweeping tide of human innovations that carried the early Church into complete oblivion beneath the weight of manmade traditions that built up the Catholic institution.

LESSON 50, 51 AND 52
A STUDY OF THE SEVEN CHURCHES OF ASIA

I. **John's Vision (Rev. 1:12-20) :**
   A. Seven golden candlesticks (v. 20), "and the seven candlesticks are seven Churches."
   B. One in the midst of them (v. 13-18). Christ in the midst of his Churches.
   C. Seven stars in his right hand (v. 20). "The seven stars are the angels of the seven churches," probably referring to the messengers of the seven Churches.
   D. A two-edged sword proceeding out of his mouth. Referring to the word delivered out of the mouth of the Lord (Heb. 4:12; Isa. 49:2; Eph. 6:17).

II. **The Meaning of the Vision:** John certainly saw a picture of the majesty and the glory of the Lord in the midst of his Church. Jesus was delivering a message to these Churches in Asia. No metaphorical or allegorical meaning can correctly be attached to these messages to these different Churches, as the Word of God gives no such meaning to them. The Churches are real, and their spiritual state is here really and literally set forth, and there is no hint or intimation that the condition of these various Churches has any reference to or connection with the Church of Christ and its state in all ages of the world as some have supposed. Such a notion is unfounded.

III. **The Churches addressed were located in cities of Asia Minor, Ephesus, Pergamos, Thyatira, Sardis, Philadelphia, Smyrna, and Laodicea, where the Gospel had been preached and the Kingdom of God established.**
While primarily intended for the Churches addressed, yet these letters are, of course, preserved that they might be of benefit to the church today. They should be, therefore, studied and the lessons applied wherever needed in the Church today.

A—THE CHURCH AT EPHESUS

(See Lesson 47 on the Ephesian Church.)

B—THE CHURCH AT SMYRNA (Rev. 2:8-11).

I. The Origin and Authority of the Message:
   A. "These things saith the first and the last, who was dead, and lived again" (Rev. 2:8).
   B. "I know." Assurance that Christ was possessed of a complete and perfect knowledge of their needs and character. His ability to direct and lead them consisted not only of a divine knowledge of the condition of the patient and the disease, but also a perfect knowledge of the remedy. The Church today cannot fail if Christ is trusted to lead.
   There is no chance of deceiving the Lord about the character and accomplishment of the Church anywhere.

II. The Character and Condition of the Church:
   A. "Thy tribulation." Smyrna was a populous city about forty miles north of Ephesus. It was possessed of a fine harbor and was a great commercial city. Idol worship was prevalent. It was possessed of a strong Jewish element and, since it was also a city under Roman rule, living a Christian life and serving the Lord was beset with many difficulties.
   B. "The Poverty." The Church actually had been made up of a membership that was extremely poor, since this is the only mention made of such a condition. A poor Church can be a strong one though. This Church existed long after the others were gone.
   "But thou art rich." They were rich in faith and good works (1 Tim. 6:18), in spite of their poverty.
   C. Enemies. "The blasphemy of them that say they are Jews, and they are not, but are a synagogue of Satan." Reproaches and bitter revilings were hurled against them because of their religion, but the Lord knew of it and would administer justice in due time. They were Jews, and yet were not Jews. This must have been true because of the principle preached by Paul (Rom. 2:28-29). Jews outwardly but not according to the Spirit or inwardly.

III. Exhortation and Encouragement:
   A. "Fear not" (Matt. 10:28). They were warned of an impending persecution but exhorted to bear it courageously through their confidence in the Lord's ability to bless them through it and fully recompense their enemies.
   B. The promised crown. "Be thou faithful unto death, and I will give thee the crown of life." There is no reason for not believing this to be a general promise. (Jas. 2:5). This not only means throughout their existence until death (Matt. 24:13), but also up to the endurance of death, if necessary, for the sake of Christ and their faith in him. "The crown of righteousness" (2 Tim. 4:8). The "crown of glory" (1 Pet. 5:4). "The incorruptible crown" (1 Cor. 9:24-25).
   C. Give heed. "He that hath an ear, let him hear what the the Spirit saith to the

churches." This is the process by which any man must come to the understanding and acceptance of the truth. Those who will not hear cannot be profited, nor can their conversion be affected (Matt. 13:14-15b).
D. The promised blessing. "He that overcometh shall not be hurt of the second death." To fail to overcome would then mean to be hurt of the second death (Rev. 20:14). A Christian then who fails to overcome will be lost.

C—THE CHURCH AT PERGAMUM (Rev. 2:12-17).

I. The Source of the Message. "These things saith he that hath the sharp two-edged sword." The message was proceeding from the Word of the Lord.

II. The Lord's Knowledge of the Church:
   A. Life, work, surroundings. The Lord knew of all. This city is said to have been the seat of emperor worship. It was so filled with wickedness that it is said to have been the location of Satan's throne. Satan held forth there and exercised control over its citizens. "I know where thou dwellest, even where Satan's throne is." The Lord is thoroughly familiar not only with our strength and weaknesses but also with our difficulties and temptations that hinder and surround us.
   B. "Thou holdest fast my name." They had not denied their confession of Christ nor had they allowed persecution to cause them to forsake their profession. They wore and honored the name of Christ, given at Antioch (Acts 11:26), and in which we can honor God today (1 Pet. 4:16).
   C. "Antipas." Evidently a martyr for faithfulness to Christ. He had been "faithful unto death." Not one worthy sacrifice or act of obedience escapes the knowledge and notice of Christ.

III. The Lord's Reproof:
   A. The doctrine of Balaam (v. 14). Error and sin cannot be tolerated in the Church. It must be corrected and put down or the influence of the Church is soon killed. The doctrine of Balaam is explained. He taught Balak to lead Israel into sin that they might be cursed for their sin. (2 Pet. 2:15; Num. 31:16). Evidently some in Pergamum were leading the saints there into sin by their teaching.
   B. The doctrine of the Nicolaitans (v. 15). Very similar to the doctrine of Balaam. At least productive of the same results.

IV. The Lord's Warning:
   A. "Repent." The guilty parties must reform. A change of purpose, determination of mind would work such a reform, if based upon godly sorrow (2 Cor. 7:10). If they did not reform, the rest of the Church would have to disfellowship them. Otherwise they would become partakers of their evil deeds (1 Cor. 5:1-8).
   B. Give heed. Christ again warns (v. 17) that they must give heed to this mes-

sage if they are to avert the punishment with which they are threatened, unless the sin spoken of is corrected.

V. **The Promised Reward.** "Hidden manna, white stone, new name." Here is indicated the (1) intimate friendship and blessings of God; (2) Full access into grace; (3) final recognition by the Lord in his glory.

D—THE CHURCH AT THYATIRA (Rev. 2:18-29).

I. **The Source of the Message. "These things saith the Son of God."**
 1. "Eyes like a flame of fire." Omniscence and penetrating nature of divine knowledge suggested.
 2. "Feet like burnished brass." Strength and omnipotence of the Lord here suggested by a metal that was a combination of gold, silver, and brass.

II. **Characteristics.** "I know thy works" (v. 19).
 A. "Charity or love." Toward God and each other as well as the poor and distressed.
 B. "Faith." Fidelity or loyalty. Faithfulness.
 C. "Service." Ministration. Most probably the work of benevolence.
 D. "Patience." Perseverance under all circumstances.
 E. "Thy last works are more than the first." They had grown in grace. A rare quality indeed. Ordinarily a revival is needed.

III. **Reproof and Admonition:**
 A. "Sufferest Jezebel." This likeness may have referred to just one character or to a group characterized by the spirit of "Jezebel" of Old Testament history. It undoubtedly is an allusion to their similarity to that disreputable character of the Old Testament (1 Kings 16:31). Her claim of being a prophetess evidently meant that she claimed some "kind of a later revelation" and to speak by divine authority. "Sufferest" means that the Church was tolerating her work and influence, when she should be put away.

 Verse 20 also describes her influence over the Church. Evidently a group had been led astray by such teaching, as had been done by the Nicolaitans and the Balaamites of the Church at Pergamum.
 B. Divine grace extended. "I gave her time to repent and she willeth not."
 C. God's patience was to end. "I cast her into a bed" and "them that commit adultery with her into great tribulation, except they repent of their works."
 D. Evil influence expurgated. "I will kill her children with death." By "children" is evidently meant those who had been influenced to practice her false doctrines. Another allusion to the Old Testament history of Jezebel and Ahab (2 Kings 10:1).
 E. Divine knowledge and justice. "I am he that searchest the reigns and hearts." Christ has repeatedly warned that he knows and cannot be de-

ceived. "And will give unto each one of you according to your works." The judgment will be one of justice in the reward of the righteous and the punishment of the wicked.

IV. Exhortation:
  A. "I put upon you no other burden." They could relieve themselves of responsibility by correcting this wrong they had been allowing.
  B. "Hold Fast." Christ will return to claim the faithful.
  C. "He that overcometh" will be exalted.
  D. "And he shall rule them with a rod of iron, as the vessels of the potter are broken to pieces" refer to the destruction of the wicked as certainly as the exaltation of the righteous has been indicated. The ambition for earthly power as a reward for righteousness that has been kindled upon the part of some certainly is not justified by this passage.

E—THE CHURCH AT SARDIS (Rev. 3:1-6).

I. A Divine Message.
"These things saith he that hath the seven spirits of God and the seven stars." Jesus possessed the Spirit in fullness or without measure (John 3:34). The message was by His authority, and the messengers of the churches (the seven stars in his right hand) were under his authority.

II. The State of the Church.
"I know thy works, that thou hast a name that thou livest, and thou art dead." Alive by reputation, reputed as a strong Church. Probably had a large membership, fine building, prominent people in its membership, etc., but dead spiritually, in faith and zeal.

III. Admonitions:
  A. "Be watchful"—Diligence.
  B. "Strengthen the things that remain"—Growth. Build upon vestige of righteousness. Cling to the faith, love, reverence, etc., which remained in their hearts. Fan these into flame.
  C. "Hold fast"—Steadfastness. Complete your works.
  D. "Repent"—Reformation.
  E. "Remember"—Gratitude.
  F. Warning—"I will come as a thief, and thou shalt not know what hour I will come upon thee." Likely referring to sudden judgment to be visited upon them for their sins.

IV. Condemnations:
  A. "A few names that did not defile their garments." Faithful and pure in their service and lives. A remnant left as leaven with which to start in recasting their character and work for the Lord.

V. Promised Rewards:
A. "He that overcometh shall thus be arrayed in white garments." Saved, redeemed. To fail to overcome is to fail to be robed in white, which unquestionably means they will be lost.
B. "And I will in no wise blot his name out of the book of life"—allowed to remain there will be among the saved. This evidences that those whose names have been recorded can be blotted out if they fail to overcome (Rev. 20:15).
C. "And I will confess his name before my Father and before his angels." This bespeaks salvation or eternal life guaranteed to those who overcome.

F—THE CHURCH AT PHILADELPHIA (Rev. 3:7-13).

I. The Writer or Author:
A. "Holy"—In whom holiness essentially dwells and from whom all holiness is derived.
B. "True"—Truth is the essence of his character. From whom all truth proceeds.
C. "Hath the key of David."
  1. Key is the emblem of authority and power.
  2. "The Key of David" is the regal right and authority of David. Jesus as the seed of David (Isa. 9:7; Luke 1:30-33; Matt. 22:41-45) had been raised from the dead to sit upon the throne of his father David (Acts 2:30-33). He is both Lord and Christ (Acts 2:36).
     Ruler over all the kings of the earth (Rev. 1:6). He is in his present position "far above all rule, authority, power, and dominion, and every name that is named, not only in this age but also in that which is to come" (Eph. 1:19-23). All of this premillennialists deny by teaching it will not take place until he comes again.
  4. "He that openeth and none shall shut." This power and authority belong exclusively to Christ and are shared with no individual or organization on this earth. Christians must recognize His authority alone. He is the "head over all things to the Church, which is His body" (Eph. 1:22-23).

II. Divine Assurance:
A. "An open door"—For the spread of the gospel.
   "None can shut"—Adversaries shall not be able to prevent it.
B. Commendation.
  1. "Thou hast kept my word"—faithfulness and fidelity to truth. No compromise with error.
  2. "Has not denied my name"—Worn and accepted no other in which to serve God. Many regard this as having very little importance, contending that a name makes no difference. They could not be thus commended.

3. "A little power"—In spite of their weakness, poverty, and small numerical strength.
4. "Because thou didst keep the word of my patience"—Their patient endurance in upholding the gospel in spite of opposition and persecution.
C. Enemies to be exposed and punished. "Behold, I will make them of the synagogue of Satan, which say they are Jews, and they are not, but do lie; behold, I will make them to come and worship before thy feet, and to know that I have loved thee" (v. 9). Those who are claiming to be the people of God upon a fleshly basis or relationship and who were rejecting others because they were Gentiles according to the flesh were to be humbled and rejected. They constituted a synagogue of Satan.
D. Shelter, divine protection. "In the hour of trial" God promises to keep them (v. 10).
E. "I come quickly" in executing judgment and retribution upon their enemies.
F. "Hold fast" in order to gain your crown or reward and not to fall short of it.

III. Promised Reward:
A. "Pillar in the temple"—Blessed in God's service and exalted.
B. "Write upon him the name of God"—An allusion to becoming a priest under Old Covenant with "Holiness of the Lord" inscribed on his forehead. It signifies identity and divine recognition.
3. Identified with "New Jerusalem" or the Church of the living God. Accepted as one of the redeemed throng.
4. "Mine own new name"—The name that Christ, the Redeemer, means to wear, and those who are faithful in his service He will acknowledge and claim before the Father.

G—THE CHURCH AT LAODICEA (Rev. 3:14-22).

I. The Preamble: Statement of authorization. Letter written by the authority of Christ.

II. Condition of Church:
A. Lukewarmness. Listless and indifferent. General conviction of the truth and importance of Christianity yet no zeal. Irresolute and undecided. Inactive and unconcerned. Here is knowledge without zeal. The Jews had zeal without knowledge (Rom. 10:2). Both are condemned and lost. Compare the condition of Ephraim and Judah (Hos. 6:4). In this condition, the Church could easily be turned either way.
B. "I would thou wert cold or hot." The most difficult person to reach is the indifferent and unconcerned. This admonition is like another— "Be a man, a good one if you can, but be a man." The greatest hindrance to the cause is the man, who, knowing the truth and his duty, will not do anything about it.
C. The Lord's attitude. Nauseated. He alludes to the known effect of tepid wa-

ter upon the stomach. It produces nausea. This is the Lord's attitude toward slothfulness, indolence, carelessness, and indifference.
D. Feeling of security and self-satisfaction. "I am rich" and have need of nothing. Supposing themselves to be all right because of the beginning they had made. Many think because they have obeyed and accepted the first principles of the Gospel of Christ they are assured of salvation.
E. Blind to their real condition—"Thou knowest not that thou art the wretched one and miserable and poor and blind and naked." There is no attitude of mind so numbing and paralyzing to the conscience as a feeling of self-satisfaction; unconscious of their true condition. As long as this remains true, there can be no improvement.

III. Divine Counsel (v. 18).
A. Seek true riches. "I counsel thee to buy of me gold refined by fire that thou mayest become rich." Wisdom from above. Faith that cannot be daunted. Grace that is unlimited. Imaginary riches always deprive one of true riches.
B. "White raiment." The righteousness of the saints (Rev. 18:8). Rather than pretense of profession, they should seek to adorn themselves with true righteousness that they might not be stripped and naked.
C. "Anoint thine eyes." To see things aright is absolutely essential to self-improvement. A man blinded by his own needs is sure to fail to seek self-improvement.
D. God reproves those whom He loves (v. 18).
E. "Repent and be zealous." Only this could correct their indifferent attitude.

IV. Divine Readiness:
A. "Behold I stand at the door and knock." Divine pleading. God is always ready to bless us when we are ready to be blessed according to His will. Readiness upon man's part to submit to the will of the Lord is the only thing needed to obtain the Lord's favor.
B. "If any man hear and open." Man's being blessed depends upon man's decision. That is always the determining factor.
C. "I will come in and sup with him." Divine aid and companionship promised as the result.

V. Divine Promises:
A. "To him that overcometh." The conquerors—not the conquered. Those who hold out faithfully have the promise, not those who backslide and fall away.
B. "To sit with me in my throne." As Christ was exalted because of His obedient suffering (Phil. 2:5-11), so He promised to exalt us when we obediently yield to the will of God and suffer for His sake.

H—SUMMARY OF THE LETTERS TO THE SEVEN CHURCHES.
I. Christ dealt with them as separate Churches. He likewise corrected and reproved them as individuals and groups within the congregation.
II. Christ commended all who were worthy and condemned everything unworthy. That is divine justice—rendering unto every man "according to his works" (Rev. 20:13).
III. Every promise given in each case was conditional. The condition being "to him that overcometh." For a man to fall by the wayside and be unfaithful cuts him off from these promises. We are kept by the power of God, but that keeping is also conditioned upon our own faith (1 Pet. 1:3-5). If our faith fails and we become unfaithful, we fall short of the promises.
IV. These Churches were in each case impressed with the divine authority upon which and by which these injunctions and instructions were being delivered. They came from Christ, and each time the address of the letter identified the source of the information therein.
V. The Lord likewise each time impressed the Churches with the importance of paying careful heed to the message in the words, "Let him that hath an ear hear what the Spirit saith to the Churches." Our salvation eventually depends upon our willingness to follow as the Spirit of God leads in His word (Rom. 8:14).